Lost Ludlow

Lost Ludlow

a collection of rare and
early photographs

RALPH BEARDMORE

LOGASTON PRESS

FRONTISPIECE: **Albumen print, Mansell and Co., *c.*1880**. The circular nave of the Chapel of St Mary Magdalene, within the inner bailey of Ludlow Castle, built *c.*1115–40. A model of the chapel, by Hereford resident George W. Gill (later Ludlow-based), was exhibited in the Fine Arts Court of the Great Exhibition of 1851. Considered an outstanding exhibit, it was purchased by the Commissioners for the Retention of Works of Ability and Ingenuity.

First published in 2023 by Logaston Press
The Holme, Church Road, Eardisley HR3 6NJ
www.logastonpress.co.uk
An imprint of Fircone Books Ltd.

ISBN 978-1-910839-66-9

Text and images copyright © Ralph Beardmore, 2023
All rights reserved. The moral right of the author has been asserted.

Without limiting the rights under copyright reserved above, no part of this publication may be reproduced, stored in or introduced into a retrieval system, or transmitted, in any form or by any means (electronic, mechanical, photocopying, recording or otherwise), without prior written permission of the copyright owner and the above publisher of this book.

Designed and typeset by Richard Wheeler in 11 on 15 Garamond.
Cover design by Richard Wheeler.

Printed and bound in Poland. www.lfbookservices.co.uk

Logaston Press is committed to a sustainable future for our business, our readers and our planet.
This book is made from FSC® certified and other controlled material.

British Library Catalogue in Publishing Data.
A CIP catalogue record for this book is available from the British Library.

CONTENTS

Preface	vii
Introduction	1
Figure List	22
Map	23
The Photographs	25
References	165

PREFACE

I first became interested in old photographs in the 1980s, at the same time that my long association with nearby Ludford House began. Inside the house was an old album full of albumen photographs, which fascinated me – and, of course, some of them are reproduced in this book.

I started visiting local salerooms with Mrs Nicholson, an antique dealer who owned Ludford House with her husband. Generally, the bread-and-butter business of these salerooms was the sale of house clearance items. Often when a house was cleared of the saleable items, anything not deemed suitable for sale was otherwise disposed of. Nearly always, a clearance would be due to a family bereavement, and, being heirlooms, family photographs were usually left to a relative's care. It's a sad fact that many families would not know who or what these old photographs represented, and many were binned.

All antique items, including any surviving old photo albums, were separated out for a special sale. Occasionally the odd flawed or damaged album would be put into a box with other assorted items in a general sale; these were end-of-sale lots with little or no value, and the boxes were often salted with flawed antiques of little value to help them sell.

One such box contained an album with a damaged cover, easily repairable. It had some labelled views of Wales, but many more were unlabelled, and, to my amazement, all were albumen views of Ludlow taken by Thomas Jones, a Ludlow photographer. This became the first item in my collection, and Thomas Jones became something of a pet project for me. Including his photographs in the book has been something of a homage.

On another occasion, an album entitled *Devon* in large gold letters, containing many early Frith photographs of Shropshire and Cheshire, came my way. Ludlow was amongst the mix; the wonderful early scenic view of Whitcliffe also features in this book.

Over time, further sales, junk shops, fêtes, jumble sales and dedicated trade fairs slowly provided more collectable items. Latterly, eBay, Delcampe Auctions, H.I.P Postcards and various other online sites have provided better buying opportunities from a vast range of diverse online dealers, a rich source of collectable items all in one place.

My first postcard, featuring Ludlow Castle, was given to me by a work colleague. Although a treasured item from his collection, being bent on Albumen prints, it did nothing to inspire me at the time, and I freely admit to having since misplaced it. Still, I gradually began to realise that many postcards carried pictures that were initially albumen photographs taken years earlier. Through these, I was introduced to the rarer locally-produced cards.

Overall, the collection has grown exponentially and now contains many of the various photograph types sold across the counter during the period spanning the 1850s until the 1940s. These include glass lantern slides, stereoviews, *cartes de visite*, cabinet cards, photogravures and collotype images. A complete set of these would carry the same photograph, but I have yet to acquire such a set.

Knowing my collection, I have never been inclined to count the total number of items I have, although I know it is huge – a fluid, amorphous thing with the occasional misplaced photograph winking at me from a dark corner.

I wanted to share some of my favourite old photographs, and hopefully the images in the book represent the flavour and diversity of the collection's content. They are arranged as a tour around the town. Other places, not too far away, also proved irresistible and have found a place in the book. The photographs

FROM THE AUTHOR'S COLLECTION

BACK ROW, LEFT TO RIGHT: cabinet book of Valentine and sons photogravure prints (Valentines were fond of 'dressing' their pictures, and the figures, including the horse-drawn cart, have all been added); album of Frith subscription albumen prints. MIDDLE ROW, LEFT TO RIGHT: *carte de visite* images, both landscape and portrait, with lantern slides in front (the portrait is of Alderman Thomas Sheppard, mayor of Ludlow in 1874 and 1884); Francis Bedford stereoviews; FRONT ROW, LEFT TO RIGHT: postcards, including a 1920s gelatin image of The Mitre Yard underwater (CENTRE)

are a cocktail of landscape, architecture and what are commonly called *animated* (that is to say, photographs that depict 'live' subjects such as people and crowds) – although 'animated' appears to be the wrong description for early photographs as groups of people were encouraged by the photographer never to move during the exposure. If they did, they would quickly blur or even disappear like wisps in the air, leaving ghosts or smudge-like marks seen on the negative; throughout the book, the odd picture with these apparitions will be seen. Knowledge of Ludlow images that are contained in many of the world's libraries and photograph archives, and gained courtesy of the internet, has become an invaluable mental reference when searching for new, rarer additions. An existential part of the collection, some of these images have inevitably made a guest appearance in the book. Hopefully, they enhance the narrative.

Introduction

Photography is the art of producing images by the agency of light
                                J.B.Schriver, 1909

The widespread availability of photographs to purchase from the mid-1800s came about with the coming together of two key events: firstly, the development of a freely available photographic medium, the patent-free collodion wet plate process in 1851; and secondly, the rapid spread of the railway system from the 1840s, which allowed easy travel and gave rise to sightseeing and tourism around the British Isles. Almost immediately, this triggered the countrywide emergence of the professional photographer in the late 1850s and early 1860s, and the commercialisation of the photographic archives they created.

So, what was this freely available collodion wet plate process that Frederick Scott Archer (1813–57) gave to the world? The main attraction of the collodion process was that a two-shilling glass plate negative could produce scores of positive copies, enabling low-cost souvenirs to be sold at a profit to eager sightseers wanting a keepsake. This revolutionary process was in contrast to earlier processes, such as the Daguerreotype, which resulted in a single positive image from each exposure. Within 10 to 15 minutes, the collodion plate could be prepared in a darkroom, exposed to the subject for a short time (often seconds), and developed to produce a negative before the plate dried. Outdoor work was possible with a mobile darkroom (lit by an orange lamp, in contrast to the red lamp used

A collodion glass plate, here inverted and placed over a blue and white lamp to show the tell-tale signs of preparation with emulsion. Gripped by tongs top-right (note the white marks left by the tongs), it was held vertically. The emulsion was applied to the plate, which was then moved about to allow the emulsion to run over the entire surface. The plate was then tilted to drain the excess from the bottom-left, shown up here by the blue lamp. Once sensitised with silver nitrate solution, it was placed solution-side toward the lens the other way up inside the camera

The pathway to photography – a nineteenth-century timeline

c.1800   Thomas Wedgewood makes the earliest attempt to capture images produced by using a *Camera Obscura* with a lens, on light-sensitive silver nitrate-coated paper or white leather.

1820s   Joseph Nicéphore Niépce creates the first photoetching in 1822, then makes 'View from the Window at Le Gras' in 1825 – the earliest surviving photograph of a real-world scene.

1830s   The process is greatly improved (with exposure times reduced from hours to minutes) by Louis Daguerre, leading to the 'Daguerrotype' by 1837. The process is patented in August 1839. Various advances made by chemist John Herschel, including the cyanotype process, 'fixing' images to make them light-fast, the use of terms *photography*, *negative* and *positive*, and the first glass plate negative in 1839.

1841   Calotype process patented by Henry Fox Talbot, following his 1835 'salt print' process. Unlike the Daguerrotype (a positive on copper made within the camera), these processes create a translucent negative, enabling multiple photographs to be printed on paper.

1848   'Albumen [egg white] method on glass' published by Niépce de St Victor (nephew of Joseph Nicéphore Niépce).

1851   Frederick Scott Archer publishes his wet plate 'collodion process', replacing the Daguerrotype as the most widely used photographic medium.

1878–   The gelatin dry plate process becomes the most widely used photographic medium. George Eastman (founder of Kodak) develops the first transparent celluloid roll film, the medium taking over from glass plates from the 1890s.

A detail from a c.1880 photograph by Francis Bedford, of the Hell Stone, Dorset, giving a rare view of the photographer's mobile darkroom in the background

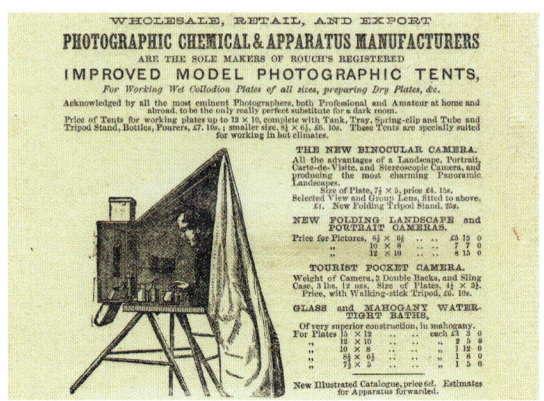

Advert from 1876 for a portable, outside darkroom, similar to that shown in the Bedford photograph (from G. Tissandier, *A History and Handbook of Photography*, 1876)

in later darkrooms), with a blacked-out coach or tent for the more inaccessible locations.

The best entrepreneurial photographers, such as Francis Bedford (1815–94) and Francis Frith (1822–98), quickly realised the potential of the new process. Their archives of images – mainly commissioned art prints, or photographic society exhibition pieces of narrow intellectual interest – were quickly expanded for public consumption. Frith in particular, who by 1860 had already set himself the target of photographing every town and village in the country, began to publish his images as souvenir photographs, and to supply them countrywide to local shops, from where they could be purchased individually or in sets. A postal shopping system was also started, whereby photographs could be obtained on approval by subscription, typically 12 per year.

Valentine and Sons, mainly Scotland-based, gained wider United Kingdom recognition after the Tay Bridge disaster of 1879, when they were commissioned to produce 50 photographs of the bridge debris for the Court of Inquiry. By 1882 they had established an extensive archive and were competing on equal terms with Frith and Co. At this time, several copy negatives could be made to increase volume, and by refreshing the negative by cropping or adding to it, the same photograph could remain on sale for several years. Valentine and Sons were adept at adding figures to the copy negative, whilst Frith and Co. frequently cropped an image or subtly erased features.

By 1860, the addition of a top layer of albumen, with a solution of silver nitrate dried onto the collodion plate, produced an easier-to-use pre-prepared, collodion dry glass plate (not truly dry, as the plate was still slightly sticky). This could be prepared a day before, with ease of use being traded off against some loss of definition and a very much longer exposure time – often in excess of 20 minutes. This made

An early tintype photograph of a little girl, *c.*1860

INTRODUCTION 5

it unsuited to portraiture, but fine as a method for photographing buildings and landscapes.

The 1870s saw the collodion process largely superseded by gelatin dry plates, with their greater convenience and reduced exposure times. However, one collodion process endured. The 'Ferrotype' or 'Tintype' involved the creation of a direct positive image onto a thin sheet of metal or tinplate. It could be quickly made, and was popular with some portrait photographers as late as *c.*1900.

COPYING OUT

The standard method of creating the final photographic print from negatives made as part of the collodion process was through the use of Albumen copying-out paper. This was a lightweight rag paper prepared with a coating of albumen (egg white mixed with salt). It was sensitised to UV light with a silver nitrate coating. The image was contact-printed (directly printed) from the glass negative onto the dried albumen coating. The copying paper was laid directly beneath the glass negative, and then both were clamped together in a frame. The image was transferred to the albumen coating on the paper when it was exposed to defused daylight (rather than direct sunlight). Once transposed, the image was 'fixed' with sodium hyposulphite which was then immediately washed off the print. The resultant thin, lightweight paper print was prone to curling, so it had to be matted to heavier paper or card for long-term keeping. To keep up with demand, printing was done on a rotating table capable of producing 10,000 images per week, or on long benches fronted by windows.

PORTRAITS AND POSTCARDS

Alongside the scenic and architectural branch of photography was studio portraiture. The introduction of the *carte de visite* in 1854 received a boost in Britain when John Jabez Edwin Mayall (1813–1901) received royal assent to publish a series of images featuring the royal family in the 1860s. People flocked to get their own portrait done, and studio work became the bread and butter of local photographers.

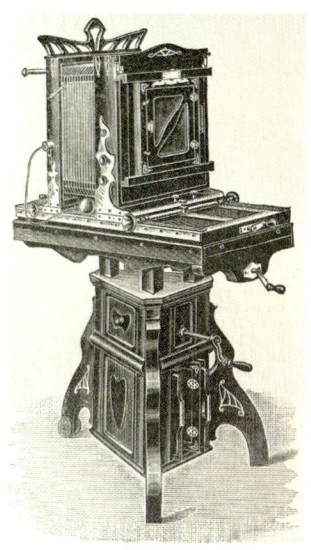

A heavyweight studio portrait camera and stand. Studio equipment was generally heavily built, partly to ensure stability during the exposure. The small image taken by this camera was capable of being enlarged to life-size. Image from *The Book of Photography*, edited by Paul N. Hasluck, 1905

A *carte de visite* group portrait of three bakers, by the Ludlow photographer Thomas Jones, c.1860–65

Portraiture was done to individual order and gave rise to a significant social change: for the first time in history, families had the chance to have inexpensive photographic portraits taken and saved into an album – something that would become the quintessential family possession of the later 1800s.

Portraiture studios were set up in suitable high street premises, with the main requirement being for plenty of natural light. Compared to outdoor photographers, who wrestled with heavy equipment and transporting hazardous chemicals, the studio environment had fewer limitations. Initially, summertime photography was preferred, not only because the season provided the optimum lighting conditions, but also comfort for the sitters. By 1860, all-year-round photography was being offered, with photographers advertising 'heated studios, conducive to every comfort'.

In 1871, The gelatin-coated dry glass plate, with greatly reduced exposure times (potentially as little as a fraction of a second), was introduced and was being mass-produced by 1878. These ready-to-use plates quickly outsold their collodion counterparts. Introduced earlier but little used until improved with a finishing layer, gelatin silver prints became popular after 1880, the pre-sensitised photographic paper becoming the new standard, replacing the albumen print (although this continued in use for a few years).

The dark tone of this photograph of the Feathers Hotel in Ludlow is typical of an early gelatin print, c.1890

The birth of the open correspondence card or 'postal' in 1870 – a stiff piece of paper or card sold pre-stamped, with half-penny postage – created a cheap way to send a written, open message. Small pictures appeared on the cards in 1894, and in 1902 the postcard as we know it was created with a printed image covering one side. Photographers with huge photograph archives, such as Frith and Co., quickly saw the potential. With considerable foresight, they switched to mechanically-printing postcards, with a process known as photolithography (the first, the 'collotype', was patented in 1855). Print-runs were initially only in the hundreds and were expensive; however, the resulting image was as good as an albumen print.

By the 1880s, the cheaper and more productive process of photogravure (pioneered by the aforementioned Joseph Nicéphore Niépce in the 1820s, and developed by Karel Klíč in 1878) was becoming more popular. Within a short time, the large photograph format had become largely obsolete as the postcard quickly became more popular, with millions selling yearly (a staggering 800 million in 1910). Towns and cities could process and deliver a postcard within 20 minutes. It was the text message of its day, quickly received and easily disposed of. However, a fondness for keeping postcards collected into albums, expressly purchased for the purpose, became part of the British psyche, which is why today millions still survive.

In 1903, George Eastman introduced the first postcard camera, the Kodak Model 3A Folding Pocket Camera. Aimed at amateur photographers, it was quickly seized upon by local professionals. It used 122 roll film with a paper backing, which produced a standard postcard-sized negative of 3¼-inches by 5½-inches. Once developed, there was no need for an enlarger or a darkroom, as contact-printing could be done in daylight by clamping the negative directly onto commercially-prepared postcard stock and leaving it to react. The postcard image could also be developed onto suitable postcard stock by exposure to a subdued artificial light source and then dipping in a developing and fixing tank.

LUDLOW AND ITS PHOTOGRAPHERS

Ludlow has many fine buildings, wide streets and much idyllic scenery, which drew in photographers from far and wide. This book contains images copied from old, original photographs, many of them now rare. They are mainly albumen silver prints from the collodion wet plate or gelatin dry plate processes; the postcards are gelatin silver prints. The glass lantern slides are either collodion or gelatin-based transparencies.

The following selection features subjects that remain popular with photographers to this day, such as St Laurence's Church and the Feathers Hotel. But while the subjects may be familiar, the passage of time can be revealing, and the earlier images are startling for their testimony of what has been lost. St Laurence's Church is pictured, showing the centuries of erosion to its stonework. The failing pinnacles atop the tower sparked a debate leading to restoration 20 years later. A hidden story emerges about the Reader's House, and the town's medieval castle is shown, ivy-clad and ruinous. Early aviators visited Ludlow, and they too have a story to tell; while the Craven Arms flying machine leads us into the tale of the earliest British flying ace recognised by American aviation historians.

The town had four publishers who sold photographs provided under licence by national photographers such as Francis Frith and Valentine and Sons. The main local landscape photographer was Thomas Jones (active 1857–1901).

Ludlow supported at least five professional photographic studios selling their wares, including portraits and postcards depicting people and local scenes and events. The individual quantities were small and initially unprofitable for large-scale mechanical printing. However, using cameras that took postcard-sized images, local studios could quickly print onto commercially-prepared rolls of postcard paper. Thus, using the old technology in a new way, images of local events could be captured, put on sale to participants, and posted countrywide within hours, if not minutes, of the event.

A mechanically-printed collotype picture, from a Valentine and Sons postcard and dated 1902, gives a rare view of publisher and printer Stones and Parker's shopfront in the New Buildings, Ludlow, on the left-hand side (now the Assembly Rooms). The shopfront display gives a sense of the popularity of the large photograph format at this time. In the display cabinet, you can see a tiny display of postcards. Within a couple of years, this type of shopfront display was a thing of the past, having been superseded by racks of postcards

NATIONAL PHOTOGRAPHERS AND POSTCARD PUBLISHERS

Francis Bedford (1816–94)
Francis Bedford was one of the earliest and most widely published photographers. Taking up photography as early as 1842, he published his photographs in books or albums throughout the 1860s, with his stereoviews forming his main output during the following decade. The quality of his work is considered peerless. Bedford constantly took pictures of the locations he loved in north Wales, the West Midlands and Devon, which he visited almost annually until at least 1884, updating or adding to his vast archive. This constant renewal is probably why another photographer, and likely his friend, Francis Frith, acquired part of Bedford's photographic library in *c*.1870.

The Library of Birmingham now holds 'The Francis Bedford Collection' consisting of 2,700 full-plate glass negatives along with 500 half-plate negatives and over 2,000 photographs.

A portrait of Francis Bedford, c.1870

William Alfred Evan Call (1878–1965)
W.A. Call was born in Paris in 1878 and was a photographer who became a postcard publisher, with hundreds of postcards and photographs to his name. He operated his photographic business from a shop where he lived in the basement. He is mainly considered a photographer of churches

and church interiors around Monmouthshire, Gloucestershire and Herefordshire. However, his output was prolific and covered many other subjects over a much wider area. In July 1939, he was invited to make the first sound and colour motion picture, but the film was lost due to the ensuing war. The war also appears to have ended his photography career.

Francis Frith (1822–98)
Francis Frith devoted himself to the new medium of photography and set up a studio in Liverpool in 1850. In 1856, he set out to record the Middle East, travelling there three times, the last time in 1859. On his return, he set up the world's first specialist photography company, Francis Frith & Co., in Reigate, Surrey. He pioneered the selling of sets of photographs by subscription. In 1860, he set out to record English villages, towns and cities, with freelance photographers carrying out the bulk of the work under contract, and catalogues of images purchased from other photographers. With a growing archive, he started to supply his

Francis Frith in Middle Eastern costume, c.1860

pictures countrywide to local outlets. From this grew the foremost company in the industry of photograph production. Today, Frith's unique archive is run as an independent business, 'The Frith Collection', after being saved from dispersal after the company's closure in 1971.

Walter Scott (1878–1946)
Walter Scott was apprenticed to photographer and postcard publisher Alfred Coe of Bakerend Road, Bradford, from where he started trading in *c.*1904. By 1905 he was firmly established, covering local events and publishing his photographs as postcards the following day. In 1920, he was at 26 North Parade in Bradford when the distinctive Walter Scott signature on his shopfront was first used on his postcards. Scott employed three photographers and 100 workers at two premises, producing postcards on rolls of paper using copy negatives adjusted to the correct size. It was not until the 1940s that the company switched to the mechanical photogravure process. The firm was sold when Scott died, but the name was retained.

William Axon Mansell (1845–1906)
W.A. Mansell – 'Photographer, photograph and bookseller, Gloucester' – was active from 1860. As well as taking photographs, Mansell collated and indexed photograph collections, both private and public, with the collections published in various books by William A. Mansell & Co. in the early 1900s. Mansell also acquired and published images from some important archives from photographers such as Emil Otto Hoppé, a widely-admired German-born portrait, travel and topographic photographer.

The Photochrom Company
The Photochrom Company was established in 1896 following the buy-out of the London office of Orell Füssli (a long-established Swiss printing company). Photochrom began mass-producing photographic cards in 1903 after acquiring the British Licence for the Photochrom process – a mechanical colour printing invented in the 1880s by Hans Jacob Schmitt of Füssli, which had set up Photochrom Zurich to capitalise on Schmitt's invention. Photochrom Co. Ltd abandoned the expensive process in 1920 for cheaper alternatives.

James Valentine (1817–79)
James Valentine started his eponymous firm in Dundee in 1851, after training in Paris. His son, William, was trained by Francis Frith and joined the business around 1860. Through William, James realised the commercial value of topographical views, and established his archive of Scottish views, selling copies to the increasingly mobile middle-class tourists. The company rapidly expanded, and opened a printing works at 152/4 Perth Road, Dundee. After James died in 1879, the business was continued by William and his younger brother George, and by 1882 the firm was taking photographs across Britain. This and their widely-distributed images from the 1879 Tay Bridge disaster, made them nationally well-known. From 1902, having perfected their in-house collotype printing process, the firm was able to use the vast archive of topographical photographs to mass-produce postcards for which they became synonymous.

Dundee City Library holds the Tay Bridge photographs, while the main photograph archive, along with other company records, is now held by the Special Collections Unit in the library of the University of St Andrews, Fife.

A portrait of James Valentine, c.1870

LOCAL PHOTOGRAPHERS

Thomas Jones (1837–c.1917)

Messrs Jones and Jones – father Robert and son Thomas – were local photographic pioneers, advertising themselves as photography artists, and selling photographs on paper and glass from 1857 until 1859 from premises in Bell Lane, Ludlow. In 1859, still with his father and calling himself a photographic artist, Thomas retailed his popular *cartes de visite* portraits at 1s each. By 1861, the pair lived at 51 Broad Street, where Thomas advertised himself as a portrait, landscape and architectural photographer, providing home visits by appointment. By late 1861 the family business had diversified, and Robert moved to nearby Leominster.

During the 1870s, Thomas often accompanied Josiah Smith, variously known as a lecturer or electrician, on his well-received countrywide touring light show extravaganzas. In March 1863 Thomas was advertising the opening of a newly-refurbished photography

In 1863, Thomas Jones collaborated with and assisted Josiah Smith, a Ludlow bookseller. This photograph, 'Girl with Dog', is an example of Josiah's work from this date

A group of farm labourers, by Robert Jones, c.1870–80

studio, heated for winter comfort, at his premises. This offered bespoke portraits of every style, priced from 1s to 3 guineas. He expanded his business, selling various photograph frames, broaches and lockets to the public, and also supplying photographic equipment and chemicals to the trade. In 1867, the British Archaeological Association chose Ludlow for the headquarters of its annual congress, and Thomas became the association's accredited photographer. By 1886 he had involved his stepson Walter and traded as T. Jones and Son, with his daughter Winifred working in the shop from about 1890.

Walter Harper (d.1932)
In 1890, Thomas Jones advertised for an intelligent boy who was required to buy himself into an apprenticeship, with the money paid being returned to the successful apprentice as wages. The lucky lad was Walter Ernest Harper, the son of Thomas's first wife's brother, with

Group portrait, from left to right: Robert Jones, Walter Jones and Thomas Jones (who was later joined in the photographic business by Walter Harper). Photo courtesy of Jill Horvath

the firm eventually becoming 'T. Jones, Son & Harper'. By 1901, the firm became 'Jones and Harper' after Thomas retired to Somerset, before moving to London in *c*.1910. From 1901 the two Walters, Jones and Harper, took several lucrative commissions providing photographs for books (something Thomas had briefly undertaken some years before). After Walter Jones died in 1909, Walter Harper continued the business at 51 Broad Street on his own, and was prolific until his death in July 1932.

George E. White (active 1920s–30s)
George White was based at 14a Bell Lane in Ludlow. Although a prodigious photographer during the '20s and '30s, no further information has so far been uncovered about his life and career.

Thomas John Evans (active *c*.1890–*c*.1920)
T.J. Evans of 5 Corve Street, Ludlow, started his business in 1895. His *cartes de visite*, although finely monogrammed with his name on the front, have plain backs. By the early 1900s,

besides postcards, he was offering a variety of photographic Christmas cards, together with miniatures in rolled gold pendants for the princely sum of 2s 6d. With advances in printing, and photographs becoming ever more widely-used in newspapers, Evans also worked as a newspaper photographer in the early 1900s.

John Harper (active 1860s)

John Harper of 133 Corve Street, Ludlow, ventured into the lucrative but competitive world of photography in *c.*1860. His father, another John Harper, operated a new and second-hand furniture business from the premises. Photographs by John are rare, and his photographic endeavours seem to have been short-lived. He eventually took on his father's business, but his son Walter was apprenticed to Thomas Jones.

A *carte de visite* portrait of a lady, by the Ludlow photographer Thomas Evans, c.1900

 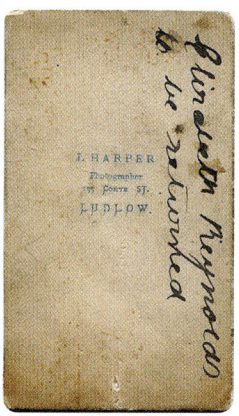

The front and back of a rare *carte de visite* portrait of a seated woman by John Harper, c.1860

W.E. Sharpe (active *c.*1880–1900)

W.E. Sharpe operated a hairdressing salon, photography studio and fancy goods and toy store from 9 and 10 Broad Street, Ludlow in the 1880s. In 1886, he also ran a business at Teme Street, Tenbury. 1895 saw him located in Castle Square. He retired in 1900.

Josiah Smith (active *c.*1860–1900)

Josiah Smith, bookseller and photographer, was another Ludlow photographic pioneer. He was based in the Castle Photographic Rooms, and his summer season photographic studio was situated at 22 Dinham. Josiah became an authority on the spectrum analysis

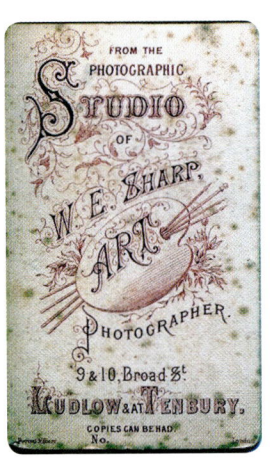

The back and front of a *carte de visite* portrait of a woman by W.E. Sharpe, c.1880

Josiah Smith's Castle Photographic Rooms were once part of this building, standing inside the castle grounds (east side), pictured here in 1890. Past uses have included a large private house and a nursery in the Second World War. It now houses a café and function rooms

A studio image by Josiah Smith of a Shropshire rifle volunteer, taken in 1860. Smith has handled the plate before it was dry, leaving several finger prints on the image

of light and other sciences, embarking on lecture tours using limelight, a kaleidoscope and an oxy-hydrogen microscope, to project scientific slides. Lectures by Josiah, advertised throughout the late 1800s in local newspapers, featured electrical storms illustrated by glass lantern slides of floundering or wrecked sailing ships. Josiah's exhibitions often included various electrical and magnetic experiments, culminating in sections of the audience receiving a mild electric shock.

Figure List & Map of Ludlow

all locations are in and around Ludlow unless italicised

Fig.	Location	Map No.
1	St Laurence's Church	2
2	St Laurence's Church	2
3	St Laurence's Church	2
4	St Laurence's Church	2
5	St Laurence's Church	2
6	St Laurence's Church	2
7	St Laurence's Church	2
8	St Laurence's Church	2
9	St Laurence's Church/ Palmers Guild College	2
10	St Laurence's Church/ Palmers Guild College	2
11	The Reader's House	3
12	The Reader's House	3
13	The Reader's House	3
14	The Reader's House	3
15	The Reader's House	3
16	The Reader's House	3
17	The Reader's House	3
18	The Feathers Hotel	4
19	The Feathers Hotel	4
20	The Feathers Hotel	4
21	The Feathers Hotel	4
22	The Bull Ring	4
23	Corve St	5
24	Corve St	5
25	Bull Ring/ King St	4 & 6
26	Bull Ring/ King St	4 & 6
27	The Bull Ring	4
28	The Bull Ring	4
29	Corve bridge	5
30	Corve bridge	5
31	Corve bridge	5
32	Corve bridge	5
33	*Queen Mary*	-
34	St Laurence's Church	2
35	The Buttercross	7
36	The Buttercross	7
37	Old Town Hall (Castle Square, High St)	8
38	Old Town Hall (Castle Square, High St)	8
39	Castle Square, High St (charabancs)	8
40	Castle Square, High St (charabancs)	8
41	Rear of postcard	-
42	Castle Lodge	9
43	Castle Square, High St (tree planting)	8
44	Ludlow Castle	1
45	Ludlow Castle	1
46	Ludlow Castle	1
47	Ludlow Castle	1
48	Ludlow Castle	1
49	Ludlow Castle	1
50	Ludlow Castle	1
51	The Linney	23
52	Dinham bridge	21
53	Dinham bridge/ mills	21 & 22
54	Ludlow Castle & Dinham mills	1 & 22
55	Whitcliffe (Bread Walk)	20
56	Whitcliffe (Bread Walk)	20
57	Whitcliffe & Dinham bridge	20 & 21
58	Mill Street weir	19
59	Whitcliffe (Bread Walk) & Ludford bridge	20 & 13
60	Whitcliffe	20
61	Whitcliffe	20
62	Whitcliffe (Bread Walk) & Ludford bridge	13 & 20
63	Whitcliffe	20
64	Ludford bridge	13
65	Ludford bridge	13
66	Ludford bridge	13
67	horseshoe weir	14
68	horseshoe weir	14
69	horseshoe weir	14
70	horseshoe weir	14
71	Bell House	15
72	horseshoe weir/ Bell House	14 & 15
73	Bell House	15
74	Bell House	15
75	Ludford House & St Giles Church	16
76	Ludford House & St Giles Church	16
77	Ludford House	16
78	Ludford House & St Giles Church	16
79	Ludford House	16
80	Ludford House	16
81	Ludford House	16
82	Ludford House	16
83	Ludford House (dance troupe)	16
84	Ludford meadows (monoplane)	16
85	*Felton Farm (biplane)*	-
86	Ludford House & St Giles Church	16
87	St Giles Church	16
88	St Giles Church (Mothers' Union)	16
89	Broad St	10
90	Broad St	10
91	Broad St	10
92	Broad St	10
93	Broad St/ Broad Gate	10 & 11
94	Broad Gate	11
95	Broad Gate	11
96	Lower Broad St	12
97	Lower Broad St	12
98	Lower Broad St	12
99	Lower Broad St	12
100	Lower Broad St	12
101	Lower Mill St	18
102	Mill St (speech day)	17
103	Upper Dinham	24
104	The Linney (Boiling Well)	23
105	*Dodmore Manor*	-
106	*Henley Hall*	-
107	*Henley Hall*	-
108	*Henley Hall*	-
109	*Henley Hall*	-
110	*Clee Hill*	-
111	*Clee Hill*	-
112	*Clee Hill (motorcyclist)*	-
113	*Hopton Court*	-
114	*Stokesay Castle*	-
115	*Stokesay Castle*	-
116	*Stokesay Castle*	-
117	*Stokesay Castle*	-
118	*Stokesay Castle*	-
119	*Stokesay Castle*	-
120	*Craven Arms*	-
121	*Bromfield*	-
122	*Bromfield*	-
123	*Bromfield*	-
124	*Bromfield*	-
125	*Oakly Park*	-
126	*Oakly Park*	-
127	*Downton Castle*	-
128	*Downton Castle*	-
129	*Downton Castle*	-
130	*Bow bridge, Downton*	-
131	*Orleton*	-
132	*Stourport (Ludlow bill poster)*	-

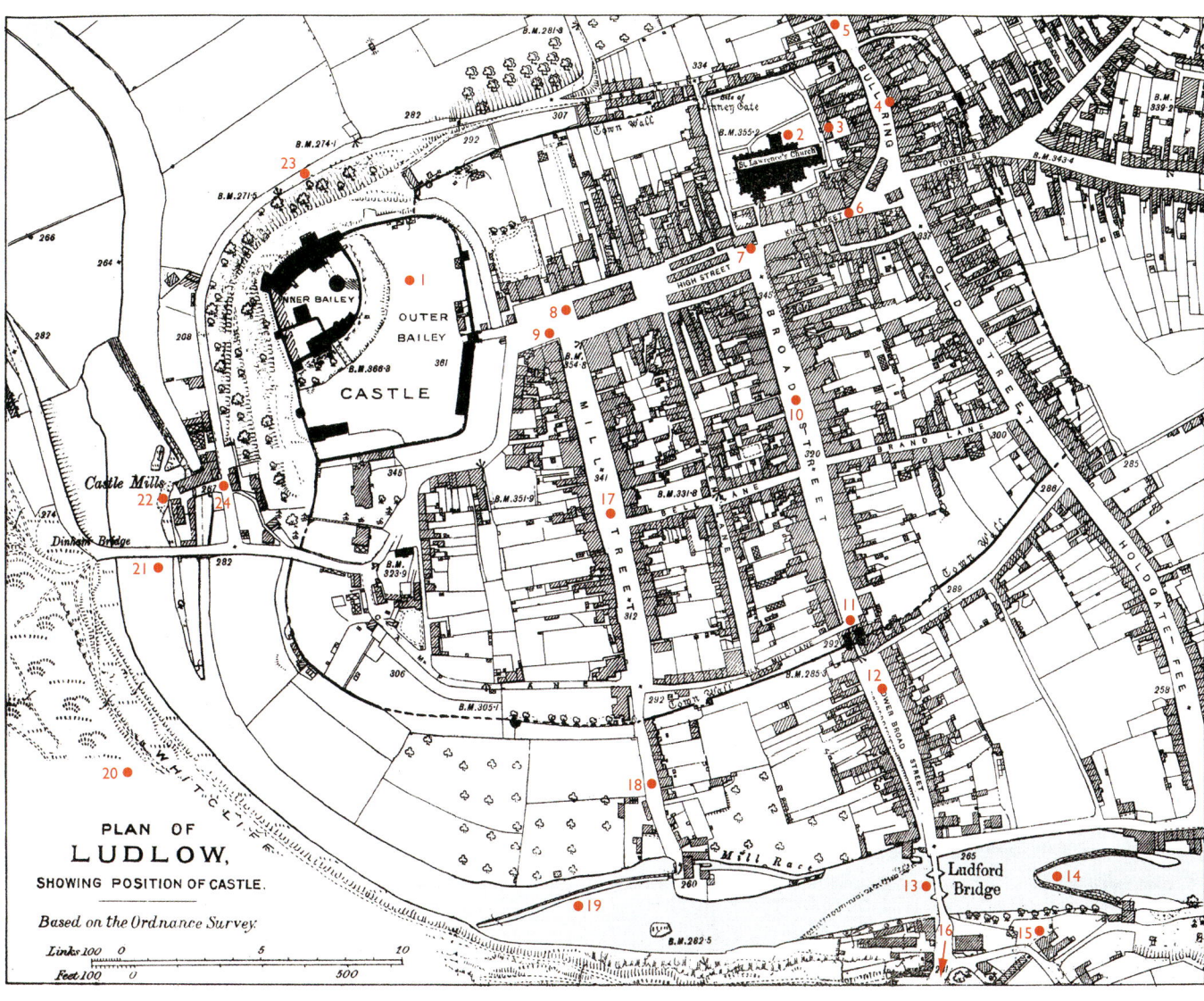

The Photographs

Fig 1 St Laurence's Church from the east
Early collodion wet plate, albumen silver print,
Thomas Jones, c.1860 or late 1850s

The antiquary, John Leland (c.1503–52) visited St Laurence's Church in 1540 and described it as 'very fare, and large and richly adornyed, and taken for the fairest in all those quarters'. Three centuries later, its stonework was in a poor state of repair. This rare photograph of the crumbling stonework of the tower and chancel was taken from a rear window on the top floor of Rickards Ironmongers, or possibly the building next door, now long gone.

The church's condition was widely known, and on 24 September 1884, a vestry meeting was held to discuss the deteriorating condition of the tower. A resolution was passed to hold a public meeting to discuss raising the necessary funds for its restoration. Time passed with no fundraising, then, four years later, a single anonymous donation of £2 10s for the 'tower restoration' in one of the collection boxes 'freely and ungrudgingly given' was the catalyst for the Grand Restoration Fund.

Fig 2 St Laurence's Church from the south-west
Detail from an albumen stereoview, unattributed but possibly by Thomas Jones, c.1865

St Laurence's Church, as seen from the upper floor of the Hosyers almshouse complex, again showing the poor state of the stonework – this time the pre-Reformation chancel of St John the Baptist and the chapel of St Edmund, with the stair turret and the porch to the right. The tower restoration was completed in 1891, but fundraising for further work continued, and even by the middle of the twentieth century there was still much to do. A *Birmingham Daily Post* article of 1956 lamented the persisting problems:

> *The beautiful Parish Church of St. Laurence, Ludlow was last night the fittingly magnificent setting for the first event of the fortnight's festival designed to help to raise another £21,000 to save the fabric of the church. An equal sum has already been spent, but much of the stonework is still in an advanced state of decay, and the persistence of the death-watch beetle threatens the ancient woodwork. The festival is planned on a scale proper to the dignity of this small Shropshire town.*

This was the birth of Ludlow's famous annual festival, which went on to feature plays by Shakespeare.

Fig 3 St Laurence's Church from the north-west
A dry plate albumen print (image no. 792), Francis Bedford, made sometime before he died in 1894

St Laurence's Church, showing the building after the restoration of the tower 1889–91. It gives a clear view in the foreground of the burial ground officially closed in 1854. Although it seems incredible for such a small area, with the traditional recycling of plots, burials were carried out here from c.1200 until 1820.

A snippet from the *Ludlow Advertiser* of February 1894 noted the following:

> The churchwardens will be in the vestry on Thursday next, February 8th, from two o'clock until four o'clock, to receive pew rents due on February 1st, plus any arrears. Applications for kneelings or notice of discontinuing any kneelings should then be given to Thomas Lowe or George Woolley, Churchwardens.

George Woolley – printer, publisher, book and fancy goods seller, trading from No. 2, the Bull Ring – advertised Bedford photographs. This image, coming from a Ludlow photograph album, may have been sold from his premises.

Fig 4 Interior of St Laurence's Church, looking east
Albumen print, Francis Bedford, dated 1863

The interior restoration of the church occurred 1859–60 when the old high-backed stalls and gallery floors on either side of the centre aisle were removed, and new pews fitted throughout. The architect George Gilbert Scott's proposed schedule of works was set out in a letter to the churchwardens, subsequently carried in the *Hereford Journal* of October 1858:

the first job is to clear it from the obstructions which now clutter and disfigure it and to refit the whole in a style and manner worthy of the noble character of the building. To this end, the fittings should be simple but massive, and of course of oak. The overhead galleries should all be removed, and I am of opinion that more really serviceable accommodation would be obtained without them. The organ should be removed from its present position above the screen, so that the chancel may be opened up to the church. The best position for the organ will probably be in one of the transepts. It is probable that some use might be made of the side chapels of the church by opening the panelling at the back of the chancel seats, which was undoubtedly originally the case. This would at least open a way for the vicar to be heard at the altar table in the aisles and transepts. The remaining works would cleanse and restore the stonework to pillars, arches, windows, etc.

By August 1860, the work was almost complete, when *Eddowes's Journal, and General Advertiser for Shropshire, and the Principality of Wales* reported that:

The extensive alterations in this noble church, which have been in progress for many months, are fast approaching completion, and the ceremony to reopen will take place on Friday next when full choral services will be performed, and sermons delivered in the morning, by the Venerable Archdeacon Waring, and in the evening, by the Hon. and Rev. George Herbert. A large number of both clergy and laity are expected to be present, and we are expressing a hope that the noble and generous efforts made by the residents of the town and neighbourhood to restore this venerable structure, one of the finest among the ecclesiastical buildings of England, will be supported on this occasion by those who admire the beautiful church or appreciate the zeal of those who have contributed to its restoration. Although, as previously said, parishioners have done much to raise funds for the present restoration, more remains to be done, for which contributions are welcome.

Fig 4

Fig 5 Chancel of St Laurence's Church
Albumen print, unattributed, pre-1870

The east window, high altar and reredos. The reredos was uncovered in 1849 when the oak screening was removed. The reordering and restoration of the interior in 1859–60 led to the congregation being moved out for a period. Services were held in the large ballroom of the New Building (The Assembly Rooms).

Damaged during the Reformation, the choir stalls on both sides of the chancel were, for many lifetimes, without their original canopies. The replacement of these canopies, intrinsic to the historic fabric, was overseen by the architect Sir George Gilbert Scott, who died in March 1878. The condition of the panelling in this image is barely discernible here due to the age-related damage to either side of the image.

Fig 6 Chancel wall monument
Albumen print, unattributed, c.1870

Fig 7 Chancel reredos
Photograph, Francis Frith and Co. (no. 30841), dated 1892

The kneeling figures are Martha and Edward Waties. Edward (son of wealthy dyer, John Waties) graduated from Oxford as a lawyer and practised his trade at the Council of the Marches, based in the castle. Waties himself had this monument installed before his death in 1635. Steeped in history, the High Chancel has several memorials dedicated to the prominent wealthy of Ludlow, who shaped the town's early history together with that of the wider Marches area.

In his book *The Parish Church of Ludlow*, published 1944, F.G. Shepherd refers to the stone reredos, found during 1849, being in a state of mutilation behind a Grecian-style altar screen of oak, in part elaborately gilded. The stone reredos was subsequently repaired by R. Kyrke Penson, FSA, church architect, with a donation by Lord Dungannon. The communion rails date from the general interior restoration of 1860.

Fig 8

T. JONES
LUDLOW

OPPOSITE: **Fig 8 View of Ludlow from the west**
Photograph, Thomas Jones, c.1865

This fine, rare view of Ludlow looks out towards the church and the site of the old collegiate buildings to the left of the church, along College Street. To the right are the buildings bordering Castle Street. The brick wall, built upon a stone rubble base running through the vegetation, remains intact today.

OVERLEAF: **Fig 9 Site of the Palmers Guild College**
Whole plate albumen photograph, attributed to Thomas Jones, c.1860–65

Another rare image, of a once long-neglected corner of Ludlow: a garden to the rear of the old college site off College Street, opposite St Laurence's, with a hotch-potch of old buildings in evident decline – the vestiges of the early medieval Palmers Guild College. To Ludlow's detriment, already in severe decline, much of this was swept away many years ago. Today, the modern College Court retirement complex occupies part of the site. The tarmac of Castle Street car park now covers the garden area. Fragments of the buildings, however, can still be found in the walls to the rear of College Street; and an interesting window in a fragment of another wall remains to the rear of the Rose and Crown public house, off Church Street. The ancient boundary wall, seen emerging from the building on the right, survives, within the Castle Street car park (albeit now unrecognisable). The site's age is discernible in the hidden higher ground level within the walled enclosure.

Described in 1886 as ruinous, this was the site of the Palmers Guild College of Chaplains. By the time of its handover to Ludlow Corporation in the mid-1500s, the college had long been home to eight chaplains, plus two others, who were affiliated to the Hosyer's Almshouses. The building fronting College Street (once part of the college but now flats) is a replacement building dating from the 1700s. This is recorded as being a private dwelling for many years before becoming Ludlow Cottage Hospital in 1874 (although the National Archives Hospital Records Database gives the founding of the hospital as 1884; it finally closed in 1982).

Fig 9

Fig 10 A game of bowls Hand-developed gelatin postcard, unattributed, c.1905

Looking the opposite direction from the previous photograph some 40 years later, a game of bowls and afternoon tea, with the castle as a backdrop. On the right, behind the trees, is the ivy-covered top of the town wall. Also just visible are chimney pots belonging to the house below the wall. Today, this tranquil lawn has become a car park.

Fig 11　　　　　　　　　　　　　　　　　　Fig 12

OPPOSITE LEFT: **Fig 11 Reader's House front elevation**
Photograph, Francis Bedford, c.1870

A photograph taken by Francis Bedford in c.1870 and later sold to the Frith Archive in c.1880. The Reader's House was a medieval stone building with a long connection to the Palmer's Guild, which used the building as a grammar school. Later, Thomas Coke (Cook), servant to Prince Arthur (who was at the castle before he died in 1502), lived there for a time, as did John Dalton, a Ludlow bookseller. A century later, from 1613, Thomas Kaye, chaplain to the Council of the Marches, radically changed the original medieval stone house into what can be seen today (Kay had obtained the lease from Ludlow Corporation, who were granted the guild's property in the mid-1500s). In 1616, this work involved demolition and rebuilding with timber framing to the rear behind the stone façade. The work was completed with the addition of this three-storied timber entrance porch over the doorway facing the church.

In the eighteenth century, the Reader's House became the official rent-free residence of the parish 'Reader', the assistant to the Rector of St Laurence's Church, from which the house took its name. After the Municipal Corporations Act of 1835, the old Palmer's Guild properties, including the Reader's House, were removed from the oversight of the Ludlow Corporation in 1837 and transferred to 17 new, Lord Chancellor-appointed trustees. The resident Reader could sublet the building, retaining any fees as part of his remuneration. In newspapers of 1909, the building was recorded as unliveable and unlived in, but was undoubtedly routinely rented for occasional use as offices or storage. In that year, after a partial internal renovation, it hosted an exhibition of crafts and antiques, borrowing a private collection to add to its exhibits, followed by permanent displays of art and antiques. For a period in the 1940s, the house was lived in by Abraham Montlake, a draper with a shop in King Street, who was fined £15 in 1942 for supplying goods contrary to the Consumer Ration Order, 1941. In 1954, very much an unspoiled, unmodernised, if perhaps slightly jaded, townhouse of the 1600s, it was granted Grade I Listed status. With the help of a grant given in 1959 towards the cost, the building, still used for perpetual exhibitions but also partly used as church offices, underwent repairs, including the replacement of timbers affected by deathwatch beetle; this was completed in 1961. With the permission of the Charity Commission, the Reader's House was sold into private ownership on 25 June 1979 by the Edward VI Charity trustees, achieving £46,000 at auction.

OPPOSITE RIGHT: **Fig 12 Reader's House rear elevation**
Hand-developed gelatin postcard, W.A. Call, c.1910

A postcard showing the rear of the Reader's House, photographed by W.A. Call, who published his postcards under the label of 'The Cambria Series' from the County Studio, Monmouth, from 1904 until the late 1930s.

TOP: **Fig 13 Reader's House interior**
Hand-developed postcard, unattributed, c.1909

By the early twentieth century, the house was in some distress. It was considered uninhabitable and described as having been empty for many years. An article about the house, written for the June 1909 edition of the *Shrewsbury Chronicle*, described partial restoration work carried out by Dodgson and Son. Also reported was a new exhibition which included interesting modern craftwork, old furniture and paintings. Antique dealer J.D. Bull loaned a pair of firedogs with grate (pictured in another old postcard), several pieces of old furniture, including a Jacobean dresser and bible box (both seen here on the left), inlaid oak chairs, a Chippendale combined bookcase and bureau, and a Georgian chair with handsome curved legs. Well furnished, the house attracted a host of visitors.

BOTTOM: **Fig 14 Reader's House interior**
Hand-developed postcard, unattributed, c.1915

Euphemistically called a museum, the Reader's House held continuous exhibitions designed to showcase art, craftwork, collectables and antiques. Whilst there were undoubtedly permanent exhibits, much of what was on show was supplied for sale by local dealers (note the ticket hanging from the dresser drawer handle).

Fig 15 Reader's House interior
Glass lantern slide photograph, A. Emone
of 2 Rockfort Place, Bath, 1936

This photograph clearly shows the unrestored and neglected part of the house, and the state of the plaster on the walls and ceiling. The chest of drawers can be seen here with a ticket on the top right drawer handle, indicating that it was probably for sale. The Reader's House was advertised in the *Ludlow Advertiser* as open to view daily. It was a good enterprise for an old house, with an added admission fee of 6d and several thousand visitors yearly.

The interior of the Reader's House is the most photographed in Ludlow, with dozens of different images by as many photographers. All relate to the contents kept or put on show, and provide a unique record of goods passing through the house at various times between 1909 and May 1955. Foxhall Antiques, the most significant contributor, emptied the house in 1955 and put all its stock up for sale over three days at its Bull Ring premises under the supervision of auctioneers Morris Barker and Poole.

Fig 16 Reader's House handlooms
Photograph of 1930, published as a postcard by the Walter Scott Company, 1941

A rare glimpse into the life of the Reader's House: a striking photographic postcard of an exhibition in the Reader's House dedicated to weaving, with two working handlooms, complimented by a spinning wheel, filling the room.

OPPOSITE: **Fig 17 Reader's House garden**
Hand-developed postcard, W.A. Call, c.1910

The enclosed garden to the rear of the Reader's House, with cobbles, crazy paving, lawn and border. The outside Victorian privy, which once stood behind the steps (and is depicted in a painting of 1872 by George Price Boyce) had been removed by the time this photograph was taken in around 1910.

This postcard is one of at least two early, numbered postcards by W.A. Call (another similar shot is numbered '55'). The title (bottom right), written onto the negative, is uncharacteristically untidy. Later titles on W.A. Call postcards were carefully added in a single line of neat writing.

Fig 17

Fig 18 The Feathers Hotel
Carte de visite photograph, Francis Bedford, c.1865

The richly timber-framed and carved main elevation of the early seventeenth-century Feathers Hotel. Its obvious visual appeal has ensured that the building has been photographed externally on more occasions than any other in Ludlow, bar the castle. The main elevation remains little-changed, and the building, now Grade-1 Listed, remains one of Ludlow's landmark buildings, and continues to be much photographed.

The landlady at the time this photograph was taken was a Mrs Prothero who continued to run the establishment on her own following the death of her husband in 1855.

In September 1929, newspapers were alive with the news that an American syndicate wanted to purchase the Feathers Hotel and remove it to the United States – although the papers also advised that the proposal would be impossible under an Act of Parliament prohibiting the exportation of ancient monuments.

Fig 19 The Feathers Hotel
Carte de visite albumen silver print, Thomas Jones, dated 1860

This photograph of the Feathers (looking north rather than south) was enlarged from an original print measuring 3.5 inches x 2 inches – a size introduced into Britain in 1857, which quickly became popular after the royal family were featured on a set of this format.

The omnibus carriage on the left, entered from the rear and with a bench seat on each side, was the hotel transport used to take customers to and from the railway station. As the railway system expanded, so its stations were fed by a willing network of posting coaches. In 1838 the railway, then in its infancy, was yet to reach as far as Ludlow, but all was not lost. 'The Railway', a 4-horse posting coach, was inaugurated, offering a service to trains at Wolverhampton. Leaving the Feathers each morning at 7 o'clock, it arrived at the New Hotel, Wolverhampton, in time for the first-class trains leaving the Wednesfield Heath Wolverhampton station, a mile from the town centre. 'The Railway' later departed from the New Hotel, returning to Ludlow immediately after the arrival of the returning trains at 4 o'clock.

With the Ludlow railway station opening to trains from Shrewsbury in April 1852, and the through-line to Hereford opening in 1853, the service ceased that year.

THE PHOTOGRAPHS 43

Fig 20 The Feathers Hotel
Kodak-type photograph, c.1950s

A remarkable and rare piece of history: a twentieth-century image of a railway porter with his handcart outside the Feathers Hotel.

While railway passengers were given a free ride to the Feathers Hotel, their luggage was always transported by a station porter using a handcart (a challenge given Corve Street's steep gradient). This was a regular occurrence dating from the opening of the station in 1852 (see the handcart and sitting railway porter in **Fig 18**).

This photograph, kindly contributed by Philip Wormington, shows his grandfather, Leonard Price (1886–1962), arriving at the hotel. Despite a gas attack during the First World War, which left him with health issues, he worked as a self-employed outdoor porter (working for tips) at the station, making the arduous trip to the top of the hill when required.

Fig 21 The Feathers Hotel Reading Room Hand-developed postcard, c.1926

This postcard, showing the Reading Room at the Feathers, was purchased at the hotel and precisely annotated on the back with: 'This is the room we had breakfast in, 2-10-26'.

Fig 22 The Bull Ring Hand-coloured collotype postcard, Valentine & Sons, c.1906

Bull-baiting took place here in the Middle Ages, and later livestock was sold here by private treaty during regularly-held animal fairs. As well as the Feathers, R.E. Crundell & Son, printer, bookseller and fancy goods supplier, can be seen on the right-hand side. If you look carefully the original print's uncoloured grey areas can be seen. Valentine & Sons spent many years perfecting their in-house collotype printing, but struggled to keep up with their competitors. Posted in 1906, the image was registered in 1896.

Fig 23 Corve Street Coloured photogravure postcard, Frith & Co. (ref. 62477), 1910

The view down Corve Street from the site of Corve Gate. The width of the town gate restricted the width of the road over which it once stood. Here the road widens again before it sweeps down the hill. The image clearly shows the condition of the town streets at the time; and the hill's steepness, as negotiated by the porter pulling his handcart full of luggage from the station below to the Feathers Hotel – a feat still undertaken several times a day until the early 1950s.

Fig 24 Parade on Corve Street Hand-developed postcard, c.1905

From the mid 1800s into the early 1900s, parades were common in Ludlow's streets, and if held on a Thursday or a Saturday the whole town could get involved (Thursdays being a shorter working day). Ludlow District Cycling Club was one of many organisations that held annual fancy-dress parades with the aim of raising funds. Postcards such as this one would have been printed and rapidly distributed in the hope of getting quick sales from those attending. Most parades traversed the town via Mill Street and Broad Street, the castle and church always playing key roles. As this parade is coming up Corve Street, the starting point would probably have been the railway station (a common route after the opening of the station in 1852).

Fig 25 The Bull Ring, looking towards King Street Hand-developed postcard, c.1904

On the left is the Tolsey, the retail premises of Francis Calver. He bought the business and a large plant nursery at Gravel Hill from a Mr Cox after moving to Ludlow in the 1870s. Mr Calver, a seedsman by trade, was an accomplished musician who could play the bagpipes and violin. A member of the Ludlow Orchestral Society, he was well-known for giving recitals, and often entertained at local events. When he passed away in February 1909, the nursery had already been sold as building plots, and part of the land became Julian Avenue.

Fig 26 King Street (The Narrows) Photogravure postcard, c.1910

Begun in 1792, W.H. Smith & Son (RIGHT) grew on the back of the expanding railway system and, by the mid 1800s, was distributing newspapers nationwide using the railway network. They also had the monopoly on selling newspapers, magazines and books on railway platforms (including at Ludlow). Papers such as the *Wellington Journal*, *Shropshire News* and *Birmingham Post* informed their railway-travelling readers where they could buy copies – often at W.H. Smith & Son. A dynamic company, it kept its workforce well-informed through its monthly magazine, *Newsbasket*; and, in just two months during 1905, after a dispute over platform rents, it opened 140 shops across Wales and the west of England – a feat probably not matched since.

Fig 27

PREVIOUS PAGE: **Fig 27 Unidentified gathering, the Bull Ring**
Hand-developed postcard, unattributed, c.1909

This is an intriguing photograph of an unidentified occasion. The unattributed image has it all: a large crowd, the mayor and other borough officials with the mace carrier and mace to the right, soldiers to the left, and the town band playing. The then mayor (Alderman Woodhouse) appears to be holding something (blurred due to the long exposure). To the left of W.H. Smith & Son is number 1 the Bull Ring – the premises of Wainwright the harness-maker, and the person in the upstairs windows is as interested as everyone else in the goings-on. Note the row of soldiers in various uniforms facing the camera. Opposite them are other uniformed men with their backs to the camera. The two rows appear to be forming a way through the crowd. The occasion is evidently an important one – almost certainly too important to be the opening of the shop behind.

W.H. Smith & Son did not open a Ludlow station franchise until 1904. In 1905, they took over Number 2 the Bull Ring, one of George Woolley's two Bull Ring premises (although it would take another two years to open). It remained the company's original store on the Bull Ring, adjoining King Street, until the 1970s. Woolley may have regretted the decision to vacate as, in 1906, an advertisement appeared in the *Ludlow Advertiser* from W.H. Smith & Son, Number 2 the Bull Ring, late of George Woolley, selling off his old stock. He resorted to issuing his own advertisement, assuring his customers that he was still in business at his main premises, number 42 the Bull Ring.

In 1907, a grand opening for Number 2 was announced. W.H. Smith's stores were all externally and internally identical. The *Ludlow Advertiser* carried the story and congratulated the company on its general fittings and shop furnishings. To achieve this accolade, the contractor gutted the ground floor, increasing the overall space by removing pillars, beams and walls. All the new fixtures and fittings were made of oak. The writer concluded that the work had been carried out to the exacting standards, fitting and appearance of hundreds of other W.H. Smith stores nationwide. (As if to amplify the *Ludlow Advertiser's* statement, the shopfront shown in this image was initially identified as a London store until its Ludlow location was confirmed through research).

Fig 28 Bull Hotel passageway
Albumen photograph, unattributed, c.1880

Also on the Bull Ring is the Bull Hotel. Perhaps the crowd seen gathered around W.H. Smith & Son in the previous image dispersed here afterwards for refreshment. This photograph shows the c.1880 toilet block in a dilapidated state. The hotel, added to and altered over several centuries, here retains its timber jettied first floor (part of a fifteenth-century five-bay rear range), probably predating the earlier parts of its opposite neighbour, the Feathers.

Many a jazz fan will have memories of the Ludlow Festival Fringe events in the yard where this toilet block once stood – including perhaps the fabulous, incomparable jazz/ blues singer and raconteur George Melly, who once took to the stage in an appropriate if grubby yellow-striped stage suit to perform. He could still ooze charm and weave his magic to enrapture the audience, albeit sitting due to age and illness.

Fig 29

River Corve in flood
Hand-developed postcards, Walter Harper, 1924

The River Corve is a tributary river forming a confluence with the River Teme upriver from Ludlow Castle. In times of flood, it can cause significant problems as it skirts Ludlow along the outer reaches of Corve Street towards the Linney via a long meander across the low-lying ground.

OPPOSITE: **Fig 29** Harper has captured the dramatic floodwaters of 1924, crossing the then Shrewsbury road leading off Corve bridge, the exit from the narrow lower end of Corve Street. In order to take this picture, Harper positioned himself on the road behind the wall, braving the floodwaters gushing from the right of this image.

ABOVE RIGHT: **Fig 30** The same flood viewed from a different angle: the telegraph pole and the long exposure hint at the speed and volume of the fast-flowing water.

BELOW RIGHT: **Fig 31** The extent of the flooding is clearly seen in this image. The course of the River Corve passes behind the industrial complex and follows the line of trees.

THE PHOTOGRAPHS   55

Fig 32 Princess Mary at Corve bridge
Hand-developed postcard, unattributed, 1909

Corve bridge was the meet-and-greet stop-off point for Princess Mary, Princess of Wales, before she toured Ludlow on 24 November 1909. The visit, a financial boost for the town, was photographed and several hand-printed postcards of the historic event were published. Beyond the car is the treeline of the River Corve, thankfully not in flood when Princess Mary arrived in her Daimler at the wide verge facing Corve bridge. Here she is being greeted by Ludlow dignitaries and townsfolk just before the bridge on her way to tour the town. The mayoress presented her with a bouquet. Individuals can be seen standing above those in front for a better view; they would have been standing on a low stone wall which is still extant.

The Earl of Powis, the princess's host for the tour, sent several letters to the town council with instructions and the princess's wishes. There were to be no flags or decorations. The princess would be seated on the right of the car. No gifts were to be presented, but she would accept a small bouquet. She would also be pleased to accept a few small unframed photographs, which she would afterwards insert into her book. She would meet the mayor briefly before entering the castle, but once inside she would only be accompanied by her entourage and guide, Mr H.T. Weyman. The *Ludlow Advertiser* of 20 November 1909 reported:

> *From information which has been communicated, by the Mayor and Town Clerk, who will meet the car. It is understood that Her Royal Highness will arrive at the Corve Street approach at noon. She will then be at the Castle at 12.15. and will drive right onto the Castle Green, where only the private party will be admitted. We understand that Mr H.T. Weyman. E.S.A. will be honoured with the duty of showing H.R.H. over the Castle. The visit to the Church will take place at 1.15 and terminate at 1.35. The royal car will lie opposite the Butter Cross, facing Old Street. The Mayor and Town Clerk will receive the Princess at the Buttercross, and she will then proceed into the Church by the West door, where the Rector will receive her. It being impossible to arrange for the school children to be marshalled on the Castle Green, they are to line Corve Street. The sides of the road will be occupied by the scholars standing about ten deep, leaving sufficient room for the cars to pass through. The route will be kept clear by a large body of extra police who will be detailed into the town for the occasion. After the visit, Princess Mary will leave by the same route to Oakly Park for lunch.*

Fig 33 Queen Mary
Coloured glass lantern slide, unattributed *c*.1910

Fig 34 Princess Mary leaving St Laurence's Church Hand-developed postcard, unattributed, 1909

Princess Mary leaving St Laurence's Church to a guard of honour by the Church Boys Brigade. The officer saluting is Captain the Revd F.H. Brown, and the person in front is either Sergeant T.W.H. Downes or Sergeant Instructor R.G. Brookes. The card explains: 'We are sending you a postcard of the Princess of Wales when she was in Ludlow last Wednesday. It is at the church door; she is shaking the hand of the Rector, Mr Woodhouse, with the Mayor standing opposite. From Aggie.' [Actually, Woodhouse was the mayor, and the rector was A.E. Lloyd Kenyon].

Fig 35 Crowd at the Buttercross, awaiting Princess Mary Hand-developed postcard, unattributed, 1909

Princess Mary's announced itinerary changed on the day. She sat on the left of her car for her drive through the town and walked to the Buttercross instead of being driven. Ludlow folk seemed to know what was to happen as a huge crowd lined the route, and this image shows a pathway through part of the crowd in front of the Buttercross being maintained by police officers. The postcard reads: 'Am sending you a photo of the crush at Ludlow – seeing the Princess of Wales last week. I am in it somewhere, but it's difficult to find me. Fond love from Frank.'

Fig 36 The Buttercross Hand-developed postcard, unattributed, c.1910–13

The Buttercross (built c.1746 to a design by architect William Baker of Audlem), this time without the crowds. In 1913 the lime plaster covering was removed from the building on the right, owned by William Bodenham. The original intention was to knock the building down and rebuild, but when the plaster was removed the quality of the well-preserved timber frame saved it. Opened in December 1888, the building further back between the two was the Birmingham and Dudley New Bank, then for many decades a branch of Barclays, until its recent closure. Four storeys high, the front was built in red and buff terracotta supplied by King and Co. from Stourbridge, and the back in Ludlow Pressed Brick made by John Sheffield at his Railway Station, Pipe and Brick Works. By 1902 the Sheffield brickworks had gone.

OVERLEAF: **Fig 37 The Victorian Town Hall**
Hand-developed Kingsway postcard, unattributed, *c*.1905

Staring down the barrel at the new town hall, prophetically described by Nicolas Pevsner as 'Ludlow's bad luck'. The town hall was built as a two-storey hall/ market with a cross-wing at each end containing the council chamber and other rooms. The foundation stone was laid in October 1888, and it opened for business in September 1889.

Unfortunately, the newly-completed building was left with severe deficiencies. In May 1892, Henry Arthur Cheers, the architect, met with the senior town councillors and Mr Richard Price, the building contractor, to discuss the problems. He admitted to poor lead flashing on the roof and agreed to put the matter right. Mr Cheers stressed that the gutters would need snow ladders. Mr Price also undertook to put lead flashing where necessary on the cross-roof of the council chamber and correct poor mortar and pointing on the gables, agreeing to replace the roof hips.

The unfinished building had a broken corbel on the market roof. Here, Mr Price merely promised to do his best to repair the unsightly stonework and repoint where necessary. There were significant gaps between the wall plates and the wall: work left unfinished, which he promised to complete by filling the gaps and replace a broken plaster panel. Price demurred to 'torch' (seal the joints between roof slates of) the roof unless it was proved that snow or rain could drive in under the slates, fearing that his workers would cause irreparable harm to the ceiling plaster beneath. He eventually agreed to the work where it was possible to gain safe access over the ceilings. Afterwards, the council approved the discussed remedial work and thanked Mr Price for his fairness.

In 1986, one year short of 100 years after the previous town hall had been demolished, the 'new' town hall was demolished having been deemed unsafe – little wonder, given its early history.

Fig 37

Fig 38 Ludlow Election 1922 Hand-developed gelatin postcard, unattributed, 1922

An atmospheric image of a large gathering in Castle Square, listening to the person speaking on the town hall balcony (on right). Annotated 'Ludlow Election 1922', no other details are given. The year 1922 saw two parliamentary elections. In January, a by-election was held following the death of the sitting Coalition Conservative (Unionist party) MP, Beville Stanier. Ivor Windsor Clive (possibly speaking from the balcony here), another Unionist Coalition Conservative, took the seat unopposed. He won the seat again in the November General Election against National Liberal, Edward Calcott Pryce.

Charabancs outside Ludlow town hall
Hand-developed sepia-toned postcards with impressed stamp for George E. White, c.1920

TOP: **Fig 39**
A large charabanc ready to take female passengers on a day trip.

BOTTOM: **Fig 40**
A smaller charabanc operated by Samuel Johnson's Supreme Motor Coach Company of Victoria Street, Stourbridge. Johnson bused people between local towns and villages, and undertook tours or day trips for both small and large groups. The group here may be a family group on a day out. Having taken a photograph, White produced at least one proof (note the pen annotation here).

RIGHT: **Fig 41**
A hastily-written note on the back of a postcard, detailing the types and prices of photographs available.

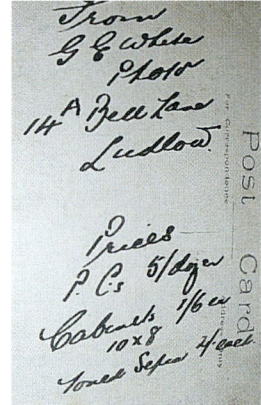

Fig 42 Castle Lodge, Ludlow Albumen *carte de visite*, Thomas Jones, 1865
(© J.P. Getty Museum Collection Picture Archive)

Castle Lodge still in its eighteenth-century livery, fully covered with lime render. Of interest are the asymmetrically-canted bay windows with plain glass. By 1890 these had been made symmetrical so that both sides were splayed. Although the window lights and glass within, dating from circa 1760, were not original features, the whole seems more pleasing to the eye than the old but non-original coloured glass on display today. Note the open drain in the road and the high pavement over a raised cobbled area, common to many of Ludlow's streets at this time. (Compare with 1902 image, p. 11)

The image on p. 11 (detail above) shows a similar view of Castle Lodge, but without its covering of lime render. Note also the altered bay windows.

In 1878, Mrs Crawford Watson was running a school for ladies, helped by 'experienced' English teachers and a French governess providing thorough English elocution, several languages, music, singing, painting and needlework. When the later image was taken, c.1902, the then proprietress, Mrs Sharp, offered classes in dancing deportment and physical culture, with indoor and outdoor exercising facilities.

THE PHOTOGRAPHS   65

OPPOSITE: **Fig 43 Tree-planting**
Hand-developed gelatin postcard, unattributed, 1905

A rare image: the ceremonial planting of an oak sapling behind the cannon near the entrance to Ludlow Castle on the morning of 9 November 1905. The occasion was to celebrate the coming of age of Other Robert Windsor-Clive, the eldest son of Lord Robert George Windsor-Clive. The ceremony was presided over by the retiring mayor Alderman Lloyd, who was presented with a silver jam spoon by Alderman Sheldon on behalf of the council. Lord Windsor had recently been made an earl and soon after this ceremony revived the title of Earl of Plymouth. He is the tall, dark figure to the fore with the top hat. Alongside him is his son, Other Robert Windsor-Clive, who sadly passed away aged 24 in 1908. (The unusual forename 'Other' is traditional in the family and derives from a legendary Saxon ancestor, 'Otho' or 'Othere').

Posted in December 1905, this hand-developed, contact-printed postcard was produced by an unknown photographer. A locally-produced image, it shows an excessive dark blue-black metallic hue created as a result of leached silvering (sugaring or mirroring) to the surface. The card, in contact with the negative, was held immovable in a frame and exposed to artificial light or daylight for a few seconds before the final development and fixing process. Surface silvering forms with age and can be removed with specialist treatment. On this particular card, one of perhaps a few dozen printed, the silvering can be seen manifested around the person planting the tree on the left. The simplicity of the developing process meant that it was used extensively by amateurs, smaller studios and professional photographers alike. This poor example highlights the variation in quality that ultimately came about. Sadly, many such cards are devoid of subject information or photographers' names.

Fig 43

Fig 44

Fig 45

OPPOSITE, TOP: **Fig 44 Ludlow Castle entrance and Crimean artillery piece**
Hand-developed sepia-toned postcard (image ref. 3569), Walter Harper(?), c.1920

A view of the main entrance to Ludlow Castle. Entering through this portal grants the visitor access into Ludlow's historical past: the castle is the very reason why the town flourished down the centuries. In the middle of the image is the Woodhouse drinking fountain (now Listed), which was presented to the town by the mayor Graham Woodhouse in 1908.

The cannon on the right is from Crimea. Its plaque reads: 'Captured 1855 at Sevastopol' – a trophy of the Crimean War 1853–6. Hundreds of captured artillery pieces, along with other metal items of value, were brought home from Russia. Many were given to towns and cities throughout England, usually by request. This gun arrived in Ludlow in November 1857. It was given for free and subsequently transported for free from Croydon by the Shrewsbury and Hereford Railway Company (perhaps because Thomas Brassey, the man running the rail company, was also one of the three men who oversaw the building of the Grand Crimean Central Railway, built to move supplies, which helped the British in the siege of Sevastopol).

The cannon was initially installed in the Market Square before being transferred to its present position two months later. A subscription paid for the plinth and iron palisade with six columns, each surmounted by a cannonball linked by an ornamental chain. Originally a ship's cannon, it was cast in 1799 at the Alexander Foundry, in the town of Petrozavodsk in Russia, under the management of Charles Gascoigne, an Englishman. It bears his inscription: D GASKION (Director Gascoigne).

Whilst many Crimea guns were given up during the Second World War (1939–45) in response to the scrap metal campaign to aid the war effort, Ludlow decided to hold on to its trophy. Instead, they donated a second trophy gun, the captured German First World War artillery piece, also displayed in front of the castle (Fig 45).

OPPOSITE, BOTTOM: **Fig 45 Ludlow Castle and First World War artillery piece**
Photogravure postcard, Photochrom Co. Ltd, 1929

This postcard shows Ludlow's captured First World War German artillery piece outside the castle, close to the main entrance. Although not seen in this image, the gun was fenced with metal railings at some point before it was given as scrap metal to the war effort in 1940.

Fig 46 Ludlow Castle outer bailey
Whole-plate albumen print from a wet collodion glass negative, Frith and Co. Ltd (image no. 30811), reg. 1892

A beautiful photograph of the outer bailey, looking north towards the Entrance Tower, Keep and Judges' Lodgings. The composition, with the lone child in the foreground, is typical of Thomas Jones, and this may have been a 'buy in' of a Jones image by Frith and Co.

A few short years after this photograph was taken, Mr Joseph Hall, a Sergeant Major with the 1st Northampton Regiment, was participating in the Tirah Campaign, the Indian frontier campaign against an uprising of the Afridi Tribe during 1897–8. He was wounded in fierce fighting in 1898 and lost a leg, and was invalided home with a pension. In 1911, the Earl of Powis appointed him as keeper of Ludlow Castle – a job he held until 1930.

Fig 47 Castle Keep and Judges' Lodgings
Albumen print, collodion dry plate, unattributed, c.1865–70

An early photograph of the castle in unkempt condition – the romanticised image so beloved of Victorian society. The overgrown state may have been tidied up occasionally. The 1859 edition of *Eddowes's Journal* reported that:

> The Archers of the Teme held their sixth and last meeting for the season within the venerable walls of Ludlow Castle Tuesday, the 30th. The day was cloudy with rain falling at intervals, and the wind being occasionally boisterous not only interfered with the shooting but also frequently displaced the targets. Nevertheless, the shooting was excellent, showing great skill on the part of several of the members.

OPPOSITE: **Fig 48 Castle Judges' Lodgings, Inner Bailey entrance and Keep**
Albumen print, unattributed, 1882

The Keep was originally a gatehouse tower for an enclosure castle, probably built or started before 1085 by Walter de Lacy before his death in that year; much of what can be seen today came later. The tower was converted into a keep in the 1200s and has been further modified since, as has much of the castle, providing more comfort and privacy. Yet more comfort was added during the Council of the Marches tenure, 1472–1679, notably with the Judges' Lodgings (left of image). This range was built in 1581, under the patronage of Sir Henry Sidney, Lord President of the Council of the Marches, 1560–86. After the Council was finally abolished in the 1600s, and with the purpose of the castle gone, its decline into ruin became inevitable. However, as late as 1777 the Judges' Lodgings were still partially roofed over.

It was reported in the *London Illustrated News*, and subsequently in national and local newspapers in January 1886, that a group of influential Shropshire people were considering buying Ludlow Castle from the Earl of Powis. The castle was then optimistically characterised as being 'not yet beyond repair', and the plan was to restore it and present it to Prince Edward Albert, Prince of Wales, as his official residence.

This image shows some of the walls of the castle in reasonable repair, but the reality was that the building was ruinous and never likely to be affordably repaired.

Fig 48

Fig 49 Ludlow Castle from the south
Albumen print, collodion wet plate, Thomas Jones(?), 1858–60

A scarce albumen photograph of Ludlow Castle, taken from an old disused quarry, possibly by Thomas Jones. In the foreground are grassy mounds, kept free of undergrowth by continuous grazing. On the extreme left, a wooded area covers the Linney fields, with rough pasture between it and the river emerging from behind the tree on the left and disappearing behind the mound on the right. Note the fissured rock face. This viewpoint was a favourite for photographers over many years, and was described in 1879:

> *The hill is marked by a clump of larches, and the most picturesque view – that which the artist would most eagerly seize for his study – is a little above these trees on the turf of the sloping hillside. The position and general character of the castle are better seen from the hilltop but we may well linger halfway down to admire the graceful outline of the far distance, the mass of towers and broken walls, the clustered leafage and the broad rushing stream that sparkles below. It is in early spring when this scene is most beautiful. The trees – oaks and sycamores – that grow on the outer bank of the castle and brush its walls are large and of some age. When the spring has not far advanced, their veil leafage scarcely hides the line of the castle walls, and yet adds grace to their ruggedness. The walls are here and there rusted with lichens and places overgrown with ivy and tufted with wall flowers. Towers with irregular and shattered crests rise at intervals. Here and there the dark rock on which the castle is founded breaks through the thin covering of turf.*

Fig 50

OPPOSITE: **Fig 50 Ludlow Castle from the south-west**
Albumen print, collodion wet plate, Francis Bedford, 1870 (acquired by Frith and Co., ref. no. 2227)

An albumen print of a similar view to the previous photograph, from a slightly different perspective. A thoughtfully-composed image photographed and published by Francis Bedford. It shows the centuries-old quarried stone of the castle standing high above, looking down upon the newly-reopened quarry, and the emergence of large 'stones' stacked in a neat pile. This image was bought from Bedford by Frith, and a stock reference photograph is held by the Victoria and Albert Museum, acquired from the company in 1954.

The photograph shows the reopening of an old quarry, a rare glimpse into how an opencast quarry was worked at this date. An entrance was formed where no underground rock was wasted as the grassy mounds were cut away to reach the fissured rock face. It would be impossible to capture this view today due to the trees and hedges that have since grown. The tree on the left is still there. The river bank is now overgrown, and a road (Dinham Road, leading to the junction with Halton Lane), has suddenly appeared. It was always there, unseen in the previous image due to the skilful camera positioning. Presumably unchanged, the iron railings along the road are still there today, now largely hidden by a hedgerow.

OVERLEAF: **Fig 51 The River Teme from Linney Meadow**
Albumen print, collodion dry plate, unattributed, *c*.1880

A picturesque photograph of the Teme from Linney Meadow, looking upstream toward Halton Lane. The river flows like a ribbon through Downton Gorge to reach this spot, then on towards Dinham bridge a mile or so downstream (off the picture, bottom left). The river is overlooked by the castle, which cradles the town in the curve of its meander as it continues its journey. Notice the neat fencing, so typical for this time.

Fig 51

OVERLEAF: **Fig 52 Dinham bridge**
Albumen print, gelatin dry plate, Francis Bedford, 1884–9

This photograph dates from after 1884 when the pinnacles on the church tower were removed for safety reasons, and 1889 when the tower restoration took place. Nestled under Ludlow Castle is Dinham bridge. Behind, the long-gabled building formed the core of the upper and lower castle corn mills, each powered by a water-driven wheel, located side-by-side at the end of the weir. By the 1800s, changes had occurred. Hodges Iron and Brass Foundry, in the buildings behind the weir to the left, was operating from at least 1844, when William Haycock, servant to Chaplin Hodges of the Ludlow Foundry, appeared before Ludlow's Petty Sessions charged with riding in a waggon without a driver. In July 1846, Thomas Hamer caught his hand in the water-operated circular saw while cutting blocks at Hodges's foundry and lost three fingers. At this time, the Upper Mill water wheel powered the foundry machinery. However, a circular saw suggests a timber mill was also operating during the early days of the foundry. The other corn mill existed on the site for a long time after. It was advertised in the *Wellington Journal* of April 1903, as having extensive premises, including a mill with seven pairs of grinding stones, warehouses, a bakery, tables and cart sheds, for let to a tenant on a 15-year lease. It was taken up by a Ludlow company, Davies and Brown, who had retail premises in Castle Street.

Being on the fringes of a town, the site suffered from inadequate sewers and poor pavements, resulting in some friction over rates. A letter from Mr Chaplin Hodges to the Mayor and Corporation of Ludlow, dated 24 October 1884, listed a number of complaints:

Living at the extreme limits of the Borough, and having my full quantity of rates to pay. I wish to draw your attention to several points that will show you that I am contributing to the rates which I receive no benefit from. Firstly, I have no paving or lighting near my premises. Secondly, I have no sewering [sic] but what I have done myself. Thirdly, I have no police officer that puts in appearance nearer than Dinham end pavement. Fourthly, no water cart to lay the dust, neither do I want one. The only benefit I receive is the Scavenger, who visits the road five or six times in the year, which would cost, I suppose, something like eighteen or twenty shillings per year. I am quite willing to pay for what benefit I receive, but to be compelled to pay something like £6 yearly in district rates for the little benefit I receive from it to my mind is a great injustice to me.

I remain, gentlemen, yours obediently,
Chaplin Hodges

The foundry buildings were finally connected to the town sewage system by 84 metres of pipe laid from Camp Lane sometime after. Meanwhile, the debt was a police matter and the subsequent non-payment of rates by Chaplin Hodges was passed to the Watch Committee, the local government body overseeing the constabulary. Chaplin's son, Robert Henry Hodges, iron and brass founder, advertised the foundry business for rent or sale in August 1889, and it continued to be advertised for rent through 1890 and February 1891. No buyer was forthcoming, so in 1892 the foundry stock in trade was sold by auction, much of it acquired by W.J. Roberts, engineer and iron founder of the Phoenix Works, Ludlow. The buildings were sold the following year.

Fig 52

Fig 53 Dinham bridge and Castle Mill
Hand-developed postcard, unattributed, c.1950–55

The remains of the Castle Mill buildings in c.1950–55. The Ludlow Electric Light Company used a mill wheel to generate electricity. The buildings, owned by Mr W.J. McCall, caught fire in 1924, destroying the roof, which was replaced with corrugated iron. In January 1926, a sealed 20-year agreement of 1906, whereby the Ludlow Corporation contracted to acquire by purchase the assets of the Electric Light Company, was acted upon. In July 1926, the borough transferred their interest to The Shropshire, Worcester and Staffordshire Power Company.

OVERLEAF: **Fig 54 Ludlow Castle and Castle Mill**
Large folio image from a 35mm negative, unattributed, 1959

In the 1950s, Ludlow residents helped raise funds to build the town's first swimming baths, here visible under construction on the Castle Mill site. The remaining mill building was turned into dressing rooms. The basic structure of the pool is in place, and groundworks are ongoing, with two men working in a trench. In the 1990s, a new pool and leisure centre was opened on a different site, making these baths redundant. Amid disquiet in the town about the fate of the site, the Dinham Millennium Green Trust was formed with the aim of saving the site from developers. Under the auspices of the Trust, what was once created by the efforts of the town's residents has been turned into a green, riverside space and kept for the benefit of its residents in perpetuity.

Fig 54

Fig 55 2nd Ludlow Regatta Hand-developed gelatin postcard, unattributed, August 1906

Ludlow's second annual regatta and swimming sports event, arranged by the Ludlow Attraction Committee and the Ludlow Swimming Club, took place on Thursday 2 August 1906. Here, spectators line the Bread Walk, spilling down to the river bank. The scene would not be possible today due to the saplings and undergrowth here, 100 yards from Dinham bridge. W. Edge won the swimming race for the Ludlow Challenge Cup. There were several sculling races for ladies, gentlemen and boys, with some well-known Ludlow families, such as the Mapps, Waits, Sweetmans and Sheldons, among the contestants. With various public health Acts, English rivers were relatively clear of sewage by the late 1800s. Ludlow's new sewerage system, completed by 1901 to enhance and replace its 1861 counterpart, meant the Teme was no exception. Messing about on rivers became a favourite pastime, and, as in other towns, regattas were routinely held in the Edwardian period and were hugely popular.

Fig 56 4th Ludlow Regatta Hand-developed sepia-toned postcard, unattributed, August 1909

Postmarked 8pm on 30 August 1909, this warm, sepia-type photograph, contact-printed on postcard paper, shows the inherent problem of photographing large groups. Some of the children moved during the exposure, resulting in the blurring of their features. Having missed a year, this photograph was taken at the 4th Ludlow Regatta, held on the 'River Teme under Whitcliffe', between Dinham bridge and Mill Street weir, on the dull, overcast afternoon of Thursday 29 July 1909. It shows the Ludlow town band conducted by Mr G. Hogan near Dinham bridge. The band played an 'attractive programme of music' during the interlude before the prize-giving ceremony.

OVERLEAF: **Fig 57 Whitcliffe and Dinham bridge**
Albumen print, collodion wet plate, image ref. 2225, Francis Frith, 1858–60

This superb image is a finely-aged 1860 albumen photograph from the camera of Francis Frith. Taken from the top of the bank, near the rocky outcrop which was destined to become the steps at the end of the Bread Walk, it captures the full majestic panorama of the Whitcliffe landscape. Dinham bridge (once called the New bridge) spans the river, an unintrusive presence in the landscape before the camera.

'The Bread Walk', the promenade along the embankment on the left of the River Teme, stretches from the bridge to Whitcliffe quarry (off camera, bottom left). Laid out just a few short years before this picture was taken, it is overlooked by the otherwise unsullied, open slopes of Whitcliffe Common: a landscape dating from the 1200s, the time of Jordan de Ludford and maintained for centuries by animals grazing on its slopes.

On the right of this is the hollow of an extinct quarry now with trees, and above this, a stand of pine trees which are still there, albeit shrouded by later woodland and undergrowth. Today, a pathway takes you through this ancient grove of pine trees. They stand above another quarry on the far side, from where so many photographers and artists captured the majestic ruins of the castle. Before the two, running up to the ridge and much older than the bridge opposite, is the well-worn track. Enshrined in ancient folklore as a packhorse trail, it was climbed by the beasts of burden carrying iron ore from Clee Hill to the Bringewood forge a few miles away. This photograph proves that the well-worn hollow-way once existed from the river crossing to the top of the hill. Today, a series of manufactured steps (known as the Donkey Steps) allows the public to climb up the lower part of the slope before the pathway turns to the right. The original track, hollow-worn into the hillside, continues upwards, but it is overgrown and forgotten today.

As if to give credence to the folk tale – if credence were needed – a large square trough, once fed by a spring, cut into the rock at the bottom, still survives. Although the spring has long since dried up, before the climb, man and beast could slake their thirst from the cool water it offered. The roughly-made trough remains as a reminder of the heavy, thirsty work the packhorses and handlers undertook before the dying embers of the forge were extinguished in c.1710.

86 LOST LUDLOW

Fig 57

Fig 58 Mill Street weir Sepia glass lantern slide, unattributed, c.1890

A lovely image of the view taken after the great flood of 1886, showing part of the Mill Street weir and the neat, tidy water's edge under the restored Bread Walk. If you look carefully at the top left-hand side of the escarpment, a group of figures can just be seen. On the rocky outcrop in the foreground, a sitting figure enjoys the view.

Fig 59 Bread Walk steps Albumen print, unattributed, c.1890

In this much-published photograph, two young boys sit on the Bread Walk steps, overlooking the riverbed and weir rising above the low water level of the River Teme. The image also affords a good view of Ludford bridge.

Fig 60 Geological Association Hand-developed sepia-toned postcard, George E. White, 1925

An image of a geological association group on a field trip, apparently in the old Whitcliffe quarry above the Bread Walk steps. With the nationwide interest in geology, associations sprang up in many towns and cities countrywide in the 1800s. Interest was accelerated by work on the sequencing and naming of rock formations by people like Conybeare and Philips in 1822, and Sir Roderick Murchison and Adam Sedgwick between 1831–39. Groups regularly travelled the country, and Ludlow's Silurian formations, arguably the spiritual home of geology, and which Murchison studied and named after the town, drew huge interest. Whitcliffe is the location of the world-famous 'Ludlow Bone Bed', now a Site of Special Scientific Interest, protected to prevent further damage by fossil hunters.

OPPOSITE: **Fig 61 Whitcliffe quarry**
Albumen print, collodion wet plate, Thomas Jones, 1865

Whitcliffe was quarried for centuries for its stone, which gave Ludlow its backbone. This image shows a deserted quarry, but it was still worked: note the neat pile of stone awaiting collection or sale. It was probably stone from here that was used on the new – and, as it turned out, troublesome – sewage beds, installed to the south as part of the town's modern sewerage system, which was completed in 1901. Very soon after, the stone, found to be unsuitable and substandard, had to be replaced.

Taken in around 1865, this photograph also shows the pristine riverside 'Bread Walk', a name shrouded in myth, laid out as a riverside promenade in 1850. The colloquial term 'Bread Walk' was rumoured to have come about from its restoration in 1886, when workmen were paid for their labours with bread and blankets. The riverside pathway, which ran from Dinham bridge, was largely destroyed in the huge floods of May 1886. Lord Clive initiated its repair. The reason for restoring the pathway was probably philanthropic, given the preceding hard winter followed by the snow and torrential rain during the spring, which left many of his men unable to work in the saturated fields. It was a long-established custom of the local wealthy, like the Clives, to provide coal, bread and blankets to Ludlow's needy during wintertime.

As work progressed, the new walkway was referred to as the 'bread and blanket path'; enshrined in folklore, it was later known locally as the 'Bread Walk'. The original made-up path only went as far as the rocky outcrop under the quarry – more or less the boundary between Lord Clive's estate and the Ludford estate owned by a descendant of the ancient Charlton family. After which, it climbed around a rocky outcrop up to the naturally worn path in the foreground. Virtually all this ground was lost to the flood, so a way was made over the rocky outcrop itself. Whatever folklore may pass on to us, the Bread Walk was mentioned by name in local newspapers before 1886 and may emanate from its 1850 construction.

Fig 61

Fig 62 The River Teme and Ludford bridge
Albumen print, gelatin dry plate, unattributed, late-1880s

From the heights near Dinham bridge, this crumpled but attractive view of the River Teme flowing towards Ludford bridge past the Bread Walk steps is overlooked by a pristine Whitcliffe common. Today, the common, rightly considered an essential and well-used amenity for the people of Ludlow, was tied to the town for centuries by its grazing rights granted to the people and burgesses in c.1220. The land granted by Jordan de Ludford and Bromfield Priory was much reduced by 1882, having been split up and partially sold off many decades earlier.

In 1901, Captain Reginald Parkinson offered the town council his manorial rights over the Whitcliffe Common for £150 and his rights to the timber growing on it for £450. The cash-strapped council entered into lengthy discussions with Captain Parkinson, holding a public meeting to gauge opinion. By the following year, Lord Windsor Clive had entered the negotiations and offered to purchase the rights to the Common and its timber. Lord Clive's intervention, with a guarantee to the council that they could apply, with his help, for conservation rights to the common and the trees on it, led to their withdrawal from the negotiations, and the sale to Lord Clive was completed soon after.

Today the common is leased to the Shropshire Wildlife Trust and maintained by 'The Friends of Whitcliffe Common', a charitable trust of volunteers who work to improve vital aspects of the 52 acres of common for the benefit of the people from the town and wider area.

Fig 63 The Bowling Green Hotel
Hand-developed postcard, unattributed, 1911

The Bowling Green was owned by Lord Windsor Clive in 1900, and situated next to Whitcliffe Common. Signed by the landlady Mrs Crane on Sunday 3 September 1911, the postcard exhibits the discolouration and leeched silvering that occurs with age on early twentieth-century postcard stock of this type. The photographer is unknown, and the title was somewhat clumsily drawn into the negative before printing.

George Warman was the landlord in 1854, and in May 1857, after a period of closure, Mr Thomas Crane, already landlord of the Bull Inn, Ludlow, took over the hotel's running. Through time, it has changed names and variously been known as the Bowling Green or, as it was in 1869 and 1885 until the turn of the century, the Ludlow Arms, and again in the 1930s. Perhaps fittingly, it was renamed the Bowling Green Inn in 1963 until it closed in 1968 under landlord Mr Turner. Today it is a private residence known as Bowling Green House.

Although not obvious here, much of the building is a seventeenth-century timber-framed structure, although it may have an earlier core. The timber frame was exposed sometime before 1936 when an up-to-date postcard of the building showing the timbers was widely available. Although no firm records exist, the structure was possibly originally conceived and built as a games lodge on the outer edges of the Charlton estate, perhaps for Job Charlton.

However, a connection with the pleasure activities of the Court of the Marches officials must also be considered. It was owned by the Charlton family and sold in c.1849 in order to settle debts. The house boasts a brick and rubble-built seventeenth-century fives court, now a Listed structure. Whilst the game of fives was largely forgotten, bowls was a hugely popular sport even before the 1800s, and the ancient bowls green that gave its name to the building, was once one of several known to have existed in Ludlow around the start of the 1900s. Many Ludlovians alive today would remember their parents or grandparents playing bowls there.

Fig 64 Ludford bridge Albumen print, collodion dry plate, unattributed, c.1870

This is a fabulous, early print of Ludford bridge from the east. Note the small tree at the corner of the Charlton Arms public house. Most local people will know this as a mature weeping willow, sadly lost in 2015.

Fig 65 Ludford bridge Monochrome postcard, Frith and Co., 1953

Many Ludlovians and local drivers will know of more recent damage to the bridge, but this Frith image, from the early 1950s, shows the sorry state of the bridge parapet. Many coping stones are missing, and a section of the wall is missing down to the level of the road.

Fig 66 Bridge group Gelatin photograph, W.E. Harper, c.1920

This poor quality image is stamped 'by Walter E. Harper' on the reverse. It was found with other photographs related to Downton Hall. The men with children on a bridge, possibly Ludford, have fishing connotations. The boy sitting with the tea can is well-shod with hobnail boots. Fourth from left is Fred Penny. W.H. Barr, a prominent Ludlow butcher annotated on the rear, is also present.

OPPOSITE: **Fig 67 Horseshoe weir from Ludford bridge**
Composite albumen print, collodion wet plate, unattributed, 1870

This superb-quality photograph represents a folio item carefully kept out of harmful daylight and away from acidic material for its entire lifetime. Taken at the height of summer from Ludford bridge, the gateway to Ludlow from the south, this image captures the seemingly motionless head of water downstream before it tumbles over the horseshoe weir below. This is a composite picture of sky and landscape: the negative emulsions of the day, while exacting perfect exposure for scenic images, always left the sky bland (due to the long exposure, the much brighter sky effectively bleached out), so initially, in the late 1860s, the sky was sometimes painted onto the negative. However, this soon gave way to conjoined, correctly-exposed negatives of the sky and scene. The idea fizzled out after 1870 as the best photographers preferred a white sky.

Even in Victorian times, conservation was actively pursued. In 1867, Mr Alexander Miller was commissioned to report to the Board of Conservators of the Seven Fisheries District on the numerous mill weirs of 'formidable character' along the River Teme and its tributaries. Of the weir at Ludford, he stated that it was 6 to 7 feet in height with a slope of 17 feet and very much in need of a fish pass, and metal grills across the mill races to prevent fish being drawn onto the mill wheels.

The weir, dating from the middle 1200s, serviced a mill on the left, at the bottom of Old Street; and two mills, possibly contemporaneous, on the opposite bank (although they may have been built slightly later). Thus, the weir may have been initially a straight diagonal from left to right, and later modified into its present form, a considerable engineering feat in either case. The weir, a Listed structure, was restored to its current condition between June and September 2002 by contractor C.J. Pearce under the direction of the Teme Weirs Trust. A fish pass was also finally incorporated into the weir to aid the annual salmon migration upstream.

Fig 67

Fig 68

OPPOSITE: **Fig 68 Horseshoe weir from Ludford bridge**
Albumen print, gelatin dry plate, unattributed, 1900

A fine if faded photograph showing the horseshoe weir and mill at Ludford. Improved glass plate and camera technology produced faster exposure times, allowing a perfect image with a natural sky.

TOP RIGHT: **Fig 69 Horseshoe weir from Ludford bridge**
Glass lantern slide, unattributed, c.1940

Hockey's Mill, on the north-east side of the horseshoe weir. Further on behind the houses is Old Street leading to the town centre. The washing on the line would suggest it was a Monday.

BOTTOM RIGHT: **Fig 70 Ludford Mill from Hockey's Mill**
Glass lantern slide, unattributed, 1860–70

A high-quality, professional glass lantern slide with near-perfect white sky. Built as a paper mill and converted to milling corn around 1868, Ludford Mill dates to c.1700, replacing two fulling mills thought to have existed as early as the mid-1200s. The building retained an internal nineteenth-century mill wheel and shaft during renovations converting it into a house. The house has since undergone modern renovation after a fire in 2011. Much of the building has been demolished since this photograph was taken. Today Ludford Mill enjoys the company of a modern hydroelectric turbine, putting green energy into the power grid.

Fig 71 Bell House garden
Glass lantern slide, unattributed, c.1920

An amateur lantern slide of a rare view of the mill and Bell House garden, as seen from the gateway onto the village, in around 1920. The wide pathway from the mill lies over part of the original medieval road coming up from the ancient ford crossing the River Teme and along the riverbank to the right and rear of the mill.

OPPOSITE: **Fig 72 Bell House from the horseshoe weir**
Albumen print, collodion wet plate, Thomas Jones, 1870

Looking towards Ludford and what is now known as Bell House, from across the dry weir. The low river level and lush vegetation tell us this is summertime. The tall ivy-covered tree to the right of the house was removed and is not seen in later photographs.

Bell House was built in the early 1600s on a medieval site, and was once part of the Ludlow Palmers Guild property portfolio. It was granted to the Ludlow Corporation in the mid 1500s. From the 1700s it was a coaching inn called The Old Bell Inn (originally licenced as The Three Crowns). In 1835, the landlord Edward Carrier sued Edmund Lechmere Charlton for loss of trade caused by the closure of the main Worcester road, running past the Bell, in favour of Charlton's 'new cutting' which diverted the road to a lane on the west side of Charlton's Ludford House. This resulted in Carrier being given a lease on Charlton's property, The Charlton Arms (known as The Red Lion until 1810) directly adjacent to the bridge. In return, Charlton took on the loss-making lease of The Bell Inn in 1839, the lease remaining with Charlton until he died in 1845.

In 1846, the Corporation, in deep litigation and subsequent financial difficulties over its Palmers Guild property, finally managed to sell the property. In the meantime, a new Bell Inn, with stabling for 80 horses, opened its doors on the other side of the river, in direct competition to Carrier's Charlton Arms tenancy. In the 1860s, building villa houses became popular in Ludlow, and it is likely that the house was renamed Ludford Villas at this time.

Fig 72

Fig 73 Bell House
Collotype print, Valentine and Sons, 1898

Bell House photographed looking south-east off Park Road in 1892 by Valentine and Sons. Entitled 'The Old Bell House', this collotype print was first published in c.1898 and showed the house as two dwellings. The image was later published as a postcard in c.1904. An article in a 1914 edition of *Country Life* described the pair of houses as having been 'base' and full of 'Victorian abominations.'

Fig 74 Bell House
Photogravure postcard, Valentine and Sons (image ref. 73961), c.1920

The Bell House in 1912. It was purchased, and the 'Bell' name, unused for many years, was reintroduced by artist Henry A. Mahler in 1909. He employed architect Basil Stallybrass to improve and renovate the property. Stallybrass, well known and well connected to the Arts and Crafts movement, discovered many hidden treasures, including wall paintings which could be as early as c.1500. Returning the property to a single unit, he removed walls and doorways, and reused authentic materials from local buildings, introducing old panelling.

The Victorian glass has gone from the windows, replaced with glass in keeping with the timber build of the period. Also gone is the two-storey bay window. The gabled dormer and porch have been replaced with a hipped dormer and larger hipped porch. Gone is the porch and entrance on the gable end.

Fig 75

PREVIOUS PAGE: **Fig 75 Ludford House and St Giles Church**
Albumen print, gelatin dry plate, Thomas Jones(?), c.1880

A well-known image of Ludford House and St Giles Church looking south, from the Ludford House photograph album. An original, unattributed whole plate albumen print of c.1880, this photograph may be the work of Thomas Jones.

The high ground behind the trees, upon which the church and Ludford House are built, marks the original property boundary, which precipitously fell away within the tree line. The wall behind the cart dates from 1835 and was built to contain some of the spoil from the new Overton Road, seen here. The original ground level is indicated by the foremost tree, planted when the area was landscaped and opened up for the new road by demolishing the turnpike house, its compound, a shed and a couple of old houses.

The brick wall on the left stands roughly where the tollhouse once stood, and the road ran further to the left of the picture, under part of the present-day Ludford Lodge, the youth hostel of c.1950. This was supposedly built as a dower house by Edmund Lechmere Charlton for his mother. However, this seems unlikely as there was some acrimony between them. As a widow, she had already remarried during the three years before Edmund succeeded to his inheritance on his 21st birthday in 1810.

OPPOSITE: **Fig 76 Ludford House and St Giles Church**
Albumen print, collodion dry plate, unattributed, 1870

Another early, unattributed photograph from an unknown family album showing St Giles Church and the north corner of the west range servant's wing of Ludford House (again, possibly by Thomas Jones). The interest of this view lies in the fact that it is an early picture of the church of St Giles, which gives a rare glimpse of the servants' wing, once a second-storey hall open to the roof.

The image was taken across the deep cutting of Overton Road from the top of the bank opposite the house. Today it is heavily overgrown, but it would not be impossible to photograph the same view from behind the two ridges in the foreground, which still survive. The large tree in the photograph still survives today, its roots anchored to the rock face upon which it stands.

Fig 76

Fig 77 Ludford House Albumen print, gelatin dry plate, unattributed, c.1885

An unattributed photograph of the north range of Ludford House, showing signs of neglect, with unpainted timbers.

Fig 78 St Giles Church and Ludford House Albumen print, Frith and Co., c.1880

This photograph of St Giles Church and Ludford House is one of a collection bought in from the photographer Thomas Polson Lugton, who retained the image for his own use.

Fig 79 Ludford House bedroom Albumen print, collodion wet plate, Thomas Jones, c.1880

This bedroom is on the first floor of the north range. Although it looks claustrophobic, it is a large and spacious room with much of the space behind the camera.

Fig 80 Ludford House oriel room
Albumen print, collodion wet plate, Thomas Jones, c.1880

The Oriel Room is a small sitting area within the large bay window attached to the north range.

OVERLEAF: **Fig 81 Ludford House**
Gelatin photograph, unattributed, c.1905

An interesting late gelatin photograph showing the ivy-covered Courthouse on the right, with lead pipes from the toilets rising above the eaves in the middle and the pipe from either the sink or bath running into the rainwater hopper on the extreme right. Modern conveniences were installed at Ludford House before 1900. The sixteenth-century hall range can be seen in the middle of the image, and the Tudor kitchen on the left.

The hatted gentleman on the right, leaning on the balustrade, is probably Mr Challoner Long, the tenant in the first years of the twentieth century. Regarding the balustrade that Mr Challoner is leaning on, this should arguably be stone. However, under magnification, this one appears to be of wood (a pegged joint is visible) and the heavyset 'cup-and-cover' turned balusters, squared at the top and bottom, are typically late Tudor/ early Elizabethan in style. Could this originate from within the house, and could it originally have been part of the Fox solar staircase once central to Job Charlton's east wing built onto the solar a century later. That particular staircase is missing, and so too is the balustrade. Sadly, this feature has long since been removed. Ludford House has a particularly complex, multi-phase building history, and this is but one of many intriguing mysteries.

Fig 81

Fig 82 Ludford House, east front Sepia-toned gelatin photograph, unattributed, c.1914–17

A rare view of Ludford House, looking across the garden from the ha-ha. Something of the splendour of the east range can be seen. The Rhododendrons are in bloom in the sunshine, indicating that it is late May or early June. Although not easy to see, a lone person stands in front of the house facing the camera whilst surveying the garden. The tranquil scene belies the 'war to end all wars' raging elsewhere, but the untidiness of the garden in the foreground is a testament to the absent men mired far away in the trenches on the Western Front.

Fig 83 Dance troupe at Ludford House
Hand-developed gelatin postcard, Walter Harper, 1932

A troupe of young dancers, probably from Miss Grace Dovey's School of Dancing. The troupe fits the description of one that took part in a dance entitled 'There are fairies at the bottom of our garden'. This was part of a larger show held in the Town Hall in April 1932, in aid of the St John's and British Red Cross ambulance car fund. If correct, the persona of the fairy queen in the middle was enacted by P. Beeson, supported by J. Tipton, D. Owen, M. Holloway, I. Langley and either J. Dixon or G. Snow. Miss Dovey, a local dance teacher and singer, produced or took part in many charitable productions, sometimes with her pupils, during the 1930s. These included at least one show put on in the grounds of Ludford House, where they often danced during the 1940s.

Fittingly, this photograph was possibly captured in Ludford's garden and by Walter E. Harper, who sadly passed away later that year. The image was made into a postcard for sale. Sold in aid of the charity, many hundreds probably still survive. The following poem, entitled *Fairy Ring*, was published in the *Leeds Mercury* in 1925:

> Let us dance and let us sing;
> Let us make a Fairy ring.
> We'll be Fairies on the green,
> Flying around the Fairy Queen,
> Swiftly Summer glides away;
> Autumn comes with colours gay;
> Winter, hand in hand with Spring,
> Dances in our Fairy ring.

OVERLEAF: **Fig 84 Bleriot monoplane on Ludford meadows**
Hand-developed gelatin postcard, unattributed, 1913

To the east of Ludford House are meadows stretching from the garden to the River Teme opposite Ludlow. A large, flat area bordering the river as far as Steventon half a mile away, it was much-used by early fliers. In 1911, Bentfield (Benny) Charles Hucks obtained his Royal Aero Club Certificate. In 1913, Hucks gave demonstration flights in his newly-acquired Blériot in the Ludlow area from Ludford meadows. For a 5/- fee, several people each got the chance to go up with him. Here, on the gentle slopes of the meadows, he is in the process of taking off in his 50hp Bleriot.

Hucks was the first British aviator to fly upside-down and to loop the loop, at Hendon Airfield in 1913. Using a special 80hp 'Looping Blériot' XI. According to the *Birmingham Daily Post* of 29 May 1914: 'Looping the loop at Ludlow, Mr B.C. Hucks (...) gave a fine display of flying from Ludford Park. Over 3,000 people attended. Mr Hucks first gave a demonstration of fancy and upside-down flying and then looped the loop several times.'

The meadows at Ludford had a history of being used as an airfield from the earliest days of flying. In an era when pilots made their way guided by sighting natural features, such as the River Teme, the open area immediately next to the town was an inviting landing area. More than one pilot in trouble made a crash landing on the meadow grass. The meadow was later registered as a temporary civil aerodrome, operated by the Berkshire Aviation Co. between February and May 1922, which gave joy-riding flights during April of that year.

OVERLEAF: **Fig 85 De Havilland biplane at Felton Farm**
Kodak photograph, C.J. Moule, Dower House, Leintwardine, 1929

On 29 September 1929, Alan Cobham, flying his De Havilland DH.61 'Giant Moth' G-AAEV 'Youth of Britain', landed on a large flat area at Felton Farm, owned by R.H. Winder, next to Ludlow racecourse. Ludlow was one stop on Cobham's gruelling Municipal Aerodrome Campaign tour of Britain between May and October of that year, and one of the 96 countrywide venues he landed at out of 107 originally planned.

Arriving at Felton at 11.30am, he was greeted by Ludlow's mayor and council officials, who were taken up for a circuit of the field having invited Cobham to attend an evening meal. Press members were then given their turn, and after landing Cobham's mechanic was called upon for minor repairs. Taking off every ten minutes and flying until dusk, he gave sponsored rides to the local schoolchildren, paid for by an anonymous donor. Afterwards, he charged anyone else to cover his costs and thereby made a small profit. Here, children can be seen boarding the plane. Alan Cobham can be seen sitting in the cockpit behind the wings.

The children's flights are now known to have been sponsored by Lord Wakefield of Castrol Oil fame. He paid Cobham to give up to 10,000 children the experience of flying during the countrywide tour.

Fig 84

Fig 85

Fig 86

OPPOSITE: **Fig 86 St Giles Church and Ludford House**
Albumen *carte de visite*, Francis Bedford, c.1865

St Giles was the patron saint of cripples and associated with leper colonies. The church is Norman in origin, though little early fabric remains. Both church and house first appear in documents in the 1200s, and the nearby leper hospital in 1275.

The overgrown church and burial ground seen here underwent a significant renovation in 1869, by local builder Mr Grosvenor, under instruction from Revd Kent, who decided against the help of an architect. The exterior was cleaned up, the walls were repaired, and some alterations made, including the removal of the nave entrance door. The plastered interior was stripped out, destroying a major part of the medieval decoration of the building.

The removal of the door was the culmination of a feud between the church authorities and Edmund Charlton some years earlier. Edmund had annexed part of the churchyard during major landscaping in 1835. Revd Kent took up his post at the invitation of Edmund in 1838, and after Edmund's death and the death of his brother Francis in 1857, and with indirect descendants living away, was free of the direct influence over his living by the Charlton family. In his 1869 renovations, funded by subscription, Kent removed the nave south entrance, compelling the congregation to use the Fox Chapel entrance on the north side. This meant that the land annexed by Edmund had to be crossed to reach it; thus, the land was returned to the use of the church by proxy. Furthermore, the Fox Chapel, the private chapel for the Ludford House occupants, became a public thoroughfare into the church.

Fig 87 St Giles Church
Albumen print, unattributed, c.1885

A much-tidied chancel and churchyard, following Revd Kent's renovations. Further acts of restoration were to follow. The *Shrewsbury Chronicle* of 29 July 1904 noted that: 'The bowl of the old font, which once stood in Ludford Church, and is now standing in the garden of Ludford House, will eventually be restored to its place in the church. At Mr C. Long's suggestion, Captain Parkinson consented to its being moved back to its rightful place.' (Mr Chaloner Long was the tenant of Ludford House at this time. Captain Parkinson was the absentee owner/ landlord).

Fig 88 Ludlow Mothers' Union Hand-developed sepia-toned postcard, stamped 'George E. White', 1932

A postcard probably taken to commemorate a special occasion, with each participant getting a copy (this copy courtesy of a member of the Nash family whose relative stands on the extreme left). The occasion is guesswork, but there are clues. There were two vicars at Ludford in 1932: Revd Edward H. Dunkley, who left in August, and Revd George Carver, who took over from him. On 20 August 1932, Mr E.H. Whitaker, on behalf of the Mothers' Union, presented Mrs Dunkley with a gold brooch. The couple at the back of the group may be Mrs Dunkley and her Revd husband after the presentation. Or, it may be Revd Carver being welcomed by the group. Revd Carver was inducted to the living on 22 October 1932 by the bishop of Hereford, under the patronage of H.E. Whitaker.

Fig 89 Broad Street Cabinet-book photogravure, Valentine and Sons, 1890

The commercial frontages on a quiet day. The buildings, still clad in lime plaster, belie the beauty of timber frames yet to be exposed. Many owe their existence to this fashionable, cheap way of building improvement. Lower down the street, the timber houses were either demolished and rebuilt or overbuilt. The wealthy who owned them built in red brick, giving the residential part of the street its distinctive Georgian look.

Fig 90 Angel Hotel, Broad Street
Coloured lithograph, Valentine and Sons (image ref. 37257), 1902

In the early to mid 1800s, the busy Angel Hotel catered for the bare-knuckle prize-fighting fraternity, who regularly stayed there. One fight recorded in 1826 was held in Ludford Park, near the deer shelters, 'commanding a most delightful prospect belonging to E.L. Charlton Esq'. The park gates were closed, and no one was allowed through without Charlton's permission. This kept the fight area secure and free of unwanted interruptions.

The fight was reported in the sporting press: 'Everything was rendered comfortable, and the fight was conducted with the etiquette of a drawing room'. In reality, the fight between Ned Neal and 'Young Dutch Sam' lasted for 77 rounds, over a period of 1 hour and 41 minutes. The fight, each round ending with a knockdown, was a bloody affair, ending in Neal being battered to unconsciousness and taken to his hotel, the Angel in Broad Street, for medical attention.

As shown here, in the first years of the twentieth century the Angel Hotel was still clad in lime plaster.

NB *Although part of the collection, this image is technically a lithograph and, unlike all of the other images in this volume, not surface-printed, and is thus something of an imposter here – though interesting nonetheless.*

Fig 91 Angel Hotel, Broad Street
Photogravure, Frith and Co. (image ref. 73784), 1923

In this photograph, taken some 20 years after the coloured lithograph opposite, the magnificent timber frame is now exposed to view. The vehicle is the hotel omnibus, used to ferry guests to and from the railway station.

OVERLEAF: **Fig 92 Broad Street parade**
Albumen print from a gelatin plate, unattributed, c.1898

This badly faded and damaged, but extremely rare, animated albumen photograph is a fascinating departure from the more familiar topographical type. It shows an assembled parade about to start down Broad Street. The large flag of St George would suggest a St George's Day parade, but on close inspection there is an overwhelming majority of children.

Over time there were many parades in Ludlow. Although pure conjecture, one description potentially fits, dated Saturday 24 September 1898. It describes a mid-afternoon fancy-dress parade by the town's youngsters, led by the Ludlow alderman Charles Wingate on horseback with a fife and drum band just behind the flag. The fancy-dress contestants are indistinguishable further behind. The contestants were judged in the evening, and prizes were awarded. The parade was flanked by young ladies collecting donations, and £11 was raised on the day.

Fig 92

Fig 93 Broad Street Hand-developed sepia postcard, unattributed, c.1913

Looking down Broad Street to the faux crenellations of Broad Gate, the last remaining of four main ancient gateways (supplemented by three postern entrances) that once allowed ingress and egress through the town walls.

Fig 94 Broad Gate Collotype postcard, G.R. Crundell, c.1910

Broad Gate as seen from Lower Broad Street, with the medieval drum tower on the left hidden by the solicitors' chambers, of c.1825.

Fig 95 Broad Gate archway
Hand-developed gelatin postcard, unattributed, c.1910

The gateway sits between the planned portion of the town behind the walls, Upper Broad Street, and the later overspill portion, Lower Broad Street. As you pass through the arch, between its two drum towers, you immediately sense the centuries of age – the worn portcullis groves on either side of you, still seen within its fabric. Seen through the archway, this group of erstwhile children appear intent on stopping marauding invaders.

As reported in *The Leominster News and North Herefordshire and Radnorshire Advertiser* in 1901, a serious bicycle accident occurred on a Saturday morning in Broad Street. A man and his wife, riding bicycles from Burnley to Cardiff, were staying in Ludlow on Friday night. On Saturday morning, shortly after 7 o'clock, they started down Broad Street, and the lady lost control of her machine, causing her to smash into the wall of Broad Gate. When she was picked up, it was found that she had broken her arm, and she was immediately taken to the surgery of Dr Strickland close by, so that her injury might be attended to. One assumes the journey was on hold after that.

Fig 96

OPPOSITE: **Fig 96 Lower Broad Street**
Albumen print, collodion dry plate, unattributed, c.1875

A superb, unmounted photograph, salvaged from a disbound album, hence the somewhat crumpled appearance. Note the midden by the bridge on the left and the open sewer opposite, typical of Ludlow streets at this time. The shadowy figure in the street is someone who unwittingly walked down the street during the several-minute-long exposure (visible coming under the arch and then in the form of three shadows along the street).

The Broad Gate, at the top of the street, was the home of John Lloyd, a prominent Ludlow solicitor. In July 1856, after the death of his first wife, Charlotte, John married a young lady named Francis (Fanny) Maria Pinhorn (the daughter of the Revd George Pinhorn, incumbent of Bromfield). Fanny naturally outlasted John, who died in 1869, living until at least 1915. Early every year from the mid 1890s, she advertised for a cook and a parlour maid. Securing reliable servants was becoming harder at this time. Fanny lived with an extended family, but the frequency of the advertisements may suggest that she was vacating the town during the winter months, possibly heading for sunnier climes.

At this time, travel abroad was popular for the local well-to-do, and steam packet travel was a lucrative tourism side-business for several Ludlow shopkeepers. As agents for various shipping companies, they advertised and sold tickets to far-flung and exotic places. In particular (and surprisingly perhaps) South America and Buenos Aires were popular destinations.

OVERLEAF: **Fig 97 Lower Broad Street**
Hand-developed gelatin postcard, unattributed, posted 1906

'When smoke stood up from Ludlow'
(*A Shropshire Lad*, verse 8, by A.E. Houseman).

The cobbles have been entirely removed from the front of the cottages on the left and replaced with stone slabs. Although a small drainage gulley can be seen, the open public drainage gully at the bottom of the street has gone. The old Bell Inn on the right-hand corner, now known as St John's House, still has its extension, which was removed a few years later when the road was widened.

This scene could have looked quite different, as in the 1820s, plans were under consideration possibly to demolish Ludford bridge and reroute Broad Street to the right. Ludlow architect Mr Stead was retained to draw up the plan, entailing most of the houses close to Broad Gate and some further down being demolished (with 41 properties potentially affected). In the event, it was decided to wait on the advice of Thomas Telford. His assessment of the bridge was better than expected, and he was subsequently responsible for easing the slope between the Broad Gate and the bridge, which survived intact. The result prompted Edmund Charlton of Ludford House to argue the case for changing the road's route, which ran on the east side of the house, to its current position on the west side. For several years he pursued the case in correspondence with Thomas Andrew Knight of Downton Castle, who, in 1825, was Commissioner for Roads and very much against the idea.

Fig 97

Fig 98 Temeside Garage, Lower Broad Street Hand-developed gelatin postcard, unattributed, 1949

An innocent photograph of people going about their business: a lady with a pram, a gentleman with a bike and someone opening their car door. Most obvious is the sign for 'Temeside Garage HE Peatt'. Horace Peatt and his wife Eveline, and their two sons Gavin and Clive, emigrated to Rhodesia (Zimbabwe) in May 1949, the year this postcard was franked. The entrance below gave access to a larger garage complex facing the River Teme, opposite Ludford bridge on Waterside Road, adjacent to the sixteenth-century St John's House.

THIS PAGE AND OPPOSITE: **Figs 99 & 100 Fulling mill fire**
Quarter-plate glass stereoview, private photographer, 1909

A fulling mill occupied a site off Lower Broad Street from as early as the 1200s and is mentioned in early documents as the Walkmill. (*waukmil* or *waulkmill*: a place to ful, meaning to cleanse cloth).

On 20 November 1811, the *Hereford Times* carried an advert for a newly-erected corn mill on the west side of Lower Broad Street, on the Walkmill site, near Ludford bridge. It announced that the whole of the machinery and interior had been put up in the last year, and there was a plentiful stream of water, with storerooms and other conveniences, now in the occupation of Mr Keysall, tenant baker, at a yearly rent of £65.

In 1842, the mill was occupied by James Hockey and advertised for sale as Teme Mill, Lower Broad Street, a corn mill with buildings and premises with a land tax worth 10d. Still occupied by Hockey, it was put on the market again in 1854 with a land tax value of 3s 10d, meaning a much-improved business and building. Hockey is better known for occupying the mill along Temeside, powered by the horseshoe weir, now more widely known as Hockey's Mill.

Refurbished and thriving, it was next advertised for sale in 1862, when it was wholly owned by Mr John Baker, this time as a woollen mill and manufactory, complete with the eight-horsepower waterwheel and all necessary modern equipment. A house, coach house and stables also occupied the large site. By the time it caught fire in July 1908, part of the complex had been demolished, and covered with a corrugated iron roof.

The mill warehouse premises were occupied by Bodenham's repository, with part sublet to J.W. Price, a wicker manufacturer. Bodenham was a significant employer in the town. Although some manufacturing may have occurred at the repository, the primary manufacturing of staple household goods was carried on elsewhere, including in premises located behind 59 Broad Street.

These photographs show the primitive equipment used to tackle fires, with wooden ladders and two firefighters sitting astride the corrugated roof to aim the hose as the pall of smoke increases. A short while after the fire, the town council decided to hire two young fit and sturdy men as firemen. The firefighters' late arrival at the out-of-control blaze also prompted a debate in the meeting about the need for an early warning fire alarm system during the daytime.

It became an unlucky building, catching fire again on 24 October 1955, when owned by Reynolds Woodware Ltd. The *Birmingham Post*, among others, reported the presence of seven brigades at the blaze. In 1977, another fire ravaged the building, and the site was purchased by Ludlow Town Council and redeveloped for social housing, regaining the historic name of Walkmill.

The fire was a significant event. Unsurprisingly perhaps, many different photographs exist. The two shown were part of a collection of 300 quarter-plate size stereoviews taken and made by an unknown photographer. From the advanced state of the fire and the position from which the photographs were taken, the photographer appears to have arrived at the scene soon after the fire started, from the general direction of the south of the town.

Fig 101

OPPOSITE: **Fig 101 Lower Mill Street**
Albumen print, collodion wet plate, Francis Frith and Co. (image ref. 2217), 1858–60

This exceptional and rare image by Francis Frith shows this part of the town in considerable detail, particularly the grammar school, seen as the gable above the trees on the left, where Mill Street narrows; and Barnaby House, with the four windows, alongside Silk Mill Lane, which the grammar school trustees eventually purchased in order to expand.

The large building backing onto the lane to the right of it is the premises of Edward C. Breeze, coachmaker, which operated from here between 1857 and 1873. Note the three figures in front of the cottages on the narrow road. It is likely that they would have been posed and asked to stand perfectly still during the several minutes exposure time – quite an accomplishment considering the distance between them and the camera operated by Frith on the high ground of Whitcliffe Common. One can imagine the frantic waving of arms signalling the start and end of the exposure time.

OVERLEAF: **Fig 102 Speech Day**
Gelatin photograph, unattributed, 1914

A school photo of headmaster H.B. Threlfall surrounded by the pupils and staff of the Ludlow King Edward VI grammar school, taken in early February 1914. At this time the school was in a predicament. Henry T. Weyman, the chairman, advised the board of governors that its finances were dire. Its income was £1,306; however, in order to meet the school's expenditure for the current financial year, £1,506 was needed. The deficit was a hangover from the monies spent on Barnaby Hall, sanctioned by the Board of Education: a capital cost but a debt nonetheless. The school had capital funds, but expenditure had to be repaid with interest, albeit on extended terms.

The county council had recommended a payment of £100 for the coming year, but Weyman thought they ought to put a more significant grant forward. There was also a need for an extra master, highlighted by the school inspectors, which would further aggravate the financial position. However, he thought the best way forward would be to encourage the council to contribute more. Mr W.H. Marston's opinion was that both expenditures resulted from external influences. He suggested impressing on the county council the need for the grant to be at least £300 to cover the Barnaby Hall repayment, plus the appointment of an extra master or mistress.

The governors agreed to write to the council, impressing on them the need for a more significant grant and for them to appoint an additional master or mistress. There was also a warning that without further financial help, the school's position would become untenable. In the event, the council agreed to an extra £100 to recruit another master or mistress.

Fig 102

Fig 103 Upper Dinham
Albumen print, collodion wet plate, Thomas Jones, 1865

Just below the grammar school is Camp Lane, which leads to the Linney and Dinham bridge. From there, one can reach the castle via the castle walk. This is a rare, early view of upper Dinham and the castle garden, dating to the early 1860s (the Getty picture archive dates the copy of their *carte de visite* version to 1865). The photograph was taken in high summer by Thomas Jones and is probably posed (interestingly, several of his photographs feature a sitting or squatting figure). This version from an album is a small square image, a stereoview-sized version of the image, and has suffered some loss of definition.

The image shows the open prospect to the front of Dinham House, and the untidy state of the road leading to the entrance, before it turns to go downhill towards Dinham bridge and the Linney (ultimately leading to Lower Corve Street). The chain and rod fence was put up after a council meeting in July 1859 when the state of the old fence was deemed ruinous, and quotes were invited for a replacement.

Henry Herbert, Earl of Powis, leased Ludlow Castle in 1772 but passed away soon after. His son, George, had the castle area landscaped inside and around the outside, resulting in the laying out of a number of paths. In 1776, George's sister Henriette, Lady Powis, directed the planting of lime trees along the new paths and in the castle garden. Several trees seen here and others elsewhere around the castle were blown down in a fierce storm on the evening of 24 October 1894.

OPPOSITE: **Fig 104 The Boiling Well**
Albumen print, gelatin dry plate, unattributed, c.1890

A rare photograph of the original wooden bridge on the well-worn pathway across the drainage channel on the River Corve flood meadows between The Linney and Coronation Avenue. The well-known 'Boiling Well' is approximately 50 metres further back in the meadow next door.

The view seen here has changed somewhat. A large mound now lies in front of the river, marked by the line of willow trees, and some of the buildings on the left are different. However, the old sewage works building, just showing on the right, still largely survives. The pathway forms a shortcut to the town. It originally led from Burway Lane, bypassing the long, Lower Corve Street loop in the days before Coronation Avenue existed, crossing a further footbridge next to a weir and leading directly to the Linney. The weir, recently removed as part of a flood alleviation scheme, once belonged to a mill that is now long-gone. The condition of the pathway across the meadow was a concern to the council surveyor in 1884, and it may well have been repaired at that time. Even so, further repairs to the footbridge were carried out in 1900, costing £2 3s, and in March 1901 the town council asked for tenders to replace it with the iron bridge we can see today.

The pathway was well-used but perhaps also notorious. In August 1899, a drunken 'E.W.' of Temeside was prosecuted for leading a frightened 8-year-old girl across the meadows. He was seen by several people who subsequently confronted him and later testified at his trial. In conclusion, the magistrate decided on a guilty verdict for technical assault as no intent could be proved, and the felon was fined 19s 6d, including costs.

John Bishop of King Street, the tenant of Boiling Well Meadow, issued a public notice in June 1895, warning people to stay on the footpath. In 1899, he was found guilty of assault against Charles Hiles of Broad Street, who had ignored the notice and walked the meadow with three dogs and a shotgun. Bishop was fined 10s with 16s 6d costs.

Fig 104

Fig 105 Dodmore Manor
Gelatin photograph, Percy Bedford (Derby), 1910

Dodmore Manor, near Ludlow, was built in the 1500s but has earlier elements suggested by the discovery of the date of 1461 carved into one of its timbers. It rested on a stone ground-floor base and was twice jettied out above this. Essentially box-framed, the timberwork was considerably enriched at ground- and second-floor level by diagonal timbers set within the square framework, giving a pattern of lozenges. A feature of Dodmore Manor was a raised diamond set within a larger diamond inset on three panels at the front of the building. The inset is also found in the timbers of the Feathers Hotel, where it is expressed as a raised head, and was also an element on Sherer's Mansion in Wyle Cop, Shrewsbury (now demolished). The houses were all once owned by officials of the Council in the Marches; Dodmore being held by Charles Foxe (d.1590), Secretary to the Council.

The earliest mention of the Dodmore estate was in the 1200s when successive male members of the Doddemore family were listed as jurors. Richard de Doddemore appeared on the founding document of the Ludlow Palmers Guild, owning land below Galdeford Gate. Dodmore eventually became the home of Richard Fisher, Alderman, three times Bailiff of Ludlow Corporation, apothecary and brother-in-law to Rees Jones, an attorney at the Council, who remodelled the Feathers in 1619. Descendants of the Nash family owned it after its purchase in 1770 by Samuel Nash. Tenant Thomas Carter farmed at Dodmore in 1850 but moved to Alcaston manor farm, a few miles away, where he retired in 1861. Fast forward to 1871, and Mr Thomas Downes of Dodmore farm won a 1st prize with his carthorse, a dark brown sire called Young Bishop, at the Shropshire and West Midland Agricultural Show at Ludford Park. In 1888, Mr and Mrs Downes passed away from smallpox. Afterwards, in late 1888 and for some years, Isaac and Mary Taylor and their four children lived at Dodmore. As the home of the Dobson family, the house appeared healthy and loved during the 1920s. However, some years later it was empty and the roof seems to have been removed, accelerating its decay before its eventual demolition in the 1950s.

OVERLEAF, LEFT: **Fig 106 Henley Hall**
Albumen print, collodion wet plate, unattributed, *c.*1874

The imposing front of Henley Hall, its roof-line animated by a gabled parapet. The hall sits just outside the suburbs of a greatly-expanded Ludlow town. Dating from at least as far back as the 1600s, it was purchased in 1770 by Thomas Knight, a member of a prominent Shropshire iron-making dynasty. He modernised the house and gardens before he died in 1803. His sister, Elizabeth, lived there until 1813. Afterwards, the Reverend Samuel Johnes (Knight) inherited. He married into the Cuyler family and eventually rented the property to his brother-in-law, Major General Sir Charles Cuyler, for a period.

Afterwards, the house was inherited by John Knight in 1853, and under his stewardship it decayed somewhat. He died in 1872, and in 1874 John Knight's executors sold the property, along with its extensive estate to Edmund Thomas Wedgewood Wood. Once again, the gardens were altered, and the house was improved by adding gabled cross-wings on the left of the house and a small extension to an existing two-storey wing on the right. In the late 1900s, the house went to the Lumsden family through marriage until it was sold in 2015.

Under magnification, a man and a woman can be seen to the right of the entrance, assumed to be the master and mistress of the house. Given the absence of the later work to the house, started in 1875, this may well be Edmund Thomas Wedgwood Wood and his wife, Sophia Louisa, posing in front of their new home in 1874.

OVERLEAF, RIGHT: **Fig 107 Henley Hall**
Albumen print, collodion wet plate, unattributed, *c.*1874

From the same date, another unattributed photograph of Henley Hall, this time showing the well-lit rear elevation. Apparently high summer, the roses in the garden are in bloom and a number of sash windows, above and to the right of the open-pedimented rear porch, have been thrown open.

On 24 March 1875, an advertisement appeared in *Eddowes's Journal and General Advertiser for Shropshire, and the Principality of Wales,*: 'Wanted bricklayers, apply Henley Hall, foreman on the work.' Obviously, the new owner at the time, Wedgewood Wood, had renovations in hand.

Fig 106

Fig 107

Fig 108 Henley Hall interior
Hand-developed gelatin postcard, unattributed, 1910

A wood-panelled interior with plasterwork ceiling and furniture from a variety of dates. The stool and wing-back chair are probably eighteenth-century; the chock-full display cabinet is characteristic of the nineteenth-century, and the roll-top writing desk from around 1900. The refectory table, on the other hand, with its elaborately-carved balluster-turned legs, may be from c.1600 (though this was a style revived in the Victorian era).

Fig 109 Henley Hall interior
Hand-developed gelatin postcard, unattributed, 1910

A second interior, this one with a painted frieze. The refectory table also appears early (possibly of c.1580), and the chair on the left (actually a backstool) is of c.1670. Note also the radiator to the left of the fireplace. The National Radiator Company Ltd (an offshoot of the American Radiator Company established in 1892) began casting radiators in Kingston-upon-Hull in 1906, with the plant expanded in 1910 (the date of this photograph).

Fig 110 Rouse Boughton Terrace, Clee Hill
Photogravure postcard, c.1930

Numbers 1–12 Rouse Boughton Terrace, showing the little village hall, now long-demolished, originally built for quarry workers in the late 1800s. The houses were sold into private ownership in 1959 by Ludlow auctioneers Morris Barker and Poole.

Fig 111 Ludlow Road, Clee Hill
Photogravure postcard, c.1930

A vivid description of travelling along the Ludlow Road, as told by Vivian Bird and published in the *Birmingham Post* on 19 March 1954: 'As we alighted on the Ludlow Road above Clee Hill village, a quarter of England lay at our feet, could we but see it. There was a tumult of wind as our vehicle was assaulted by solid rods of rain as we chugged remorselessly uphill. Then came the cloud base, fantastic vaporous shapes leaping the road from hedgerow to hedgerow, and ultimately complete envelopment'.

Fig 112 Motorcyclist Kodak photograph, unattributed, 1926

A lady on a 1924 2.34 side-valve BSA motorcycle – an image evocative of the early lady pioneers of the road, such as Dorothy Levitt at the dawn of the twentieth century. It is annotated: 'On the Clee Hills on route to Ludlow, July 1926'. The BK Portsmouth licence plate registration was issued for 21 years, from December 1903 to 1924.

Fig 113 Hopton Court Hand-developed gelatin postcard, unattributed, c.1910

A fine image of Hopton Court, with other cameramen present, possibly indicating an event is taking place. Vice-Admiral Robert Woodward, C.B., R.N. had died in 1907, so the owner at this time was Robert Woodward, his son. A large sale of Hopton Court contents occurred in October 1963. Listed were 2,000 ounces of silver, 300 dozen bottles of fine wine, 87 paintings, framed engravings and 1,200 books, along with small furniture items. Today, Hopton Court is home to an entertainment business catering for corporate events, weddings, music festivals and the local point-to-point.

Fig 114

Fig 115

146　LOST LUDLOW

OPPOSITE, LEFT: **Fig 114 Stokesay Castle north tower**
Salt paper print, Amelia Elizabeth Guppy (though possibly William Russell Sedgefield, 1850), 1854, (J.P. Getty Museum Collection, courtesy of the Getty open content programme)

By the early 1800s and after generations of subletting to the nearby farmer, Stokesay Castle, a medieval fortified house dating from the 1200s, was in a ruinous condition. Antiquarian John Britton noted in 1813 that the building had been 'abandoned to neglect'. The condition of the building had not been helped by a fire that gutted the south tower in 1830. To some extent, it was eventually repaired by the then-owner Lord William Craven, who re-roofed the tower in 1853.

The Getty Archive has Amelia Elizabeth Guppy (1808–86), a pioneering photographer, painter and explorer, and much more besides, as the photographer for both images. She was born in Hertfordshire, married at Bitterly Court, Shropshire and moved to Trinidad with her husband. She regularly visited England and amassed a large photograph negative archive, which was badly stored and perished in the Second World War. Images of Stokesay Castle photographed from the churchyard, however, survived.

Although the Getty Archive lists this photograph as being by Amelia Elizabeth Guppy, the Reading Museum holds a salt print copy of one of the images (ref. no. REDMG: 2001.304.16), dated by them to 1850 and attributed not to Guppy but to William Russell Sedgefield. In it, the standing female bears a striking similarity to an unattributed *carte de visite* portrait image of Amelia held in the National Portrait Gallery (ref. NPG x200115).

William Russell Sedgefield started out an amateur photographer. He baulked at the licence fee of £20 to use Henry Fox Talbot's patented Calotype process, and used the method regardless. He later became a highly-respected and critically-acclaimed photographer who counted Francis Frith as one of his friends. It is feasible that Amelia was also in his circle of friends and that he took the photograph of her against the background of Stokesay.

OPPOSITE, RIGHT: **Fig 115 Stokesay Castle north tower**
Salt paper print, Amelia Elizabeth Guppy, 1854 (J.P. Getty Museum Collection, courtesy of the Getty open content programme)

A very similar view of the ruinous state of the north tower midway through the nineteenth century, albeit taken from slightly further round to the east. In this photograph the apparently burnt timbers are more prevalent, particularly on the projecting bay. The roof appears to be in good condition, and the north tower may have recently been re-roofed.

OPPOSITE: **Fig 116 Stokesay Castle**
Albumen print, dry gelatin plate, Thomas Jones, c.1880

A day out at Stokesay Castle, photographed by Thomas Jones in around 1880. Note the two little heads peering out of the opposite window of the south tower. Such trips were usually organised by a local society for the benefit of its members. Jones's photographic skills are evident here: to get such a large gathering to remain still for the time required to take this image was no mean feat.

In 1869 the following advertisement appeared in local and national newspapers:

> For sale, the Stokesay Castle, an important freehold domain, comprising the manors of Culmington, Onibury, and Stokesay, 15 first-class farms, three inns, mills, numerous cottages, the whole embracing an area of 5,200 acres, producing the annual value of about £27,500: Also, the Advowson [nomination of the vicar] to the Living of Onibury.

Stokesay was purchased by John Derby Allcroft, managing director of the part-owned family firm of Dent Allcroft and Co., London, leather glove makers. A philanthropist and devout evangelical Christian, he was responsible for building several London churches and a hospital, and was also responsible for building Stokesay Court at Onibury, completed in 1892. Stokesay Castle has a long history of alterations, renovations and repairs, including some 'slighting' during the English Civil War. Fire had all but destroyed much of the south tower internal timberwork.

In the days before the National Trust, Listing Buildings and local government preservation orders, Allcroft instigated repairs and historically accurate renovations to the dilapidated fabric, all at his own expense. As such, he is responsible for its apparently unchanged medieval/ seventeenth-century appearance, and its survival to the present day.

In 1890, a destructive fire, ignited by a passing train, burned 19 ricks of straw and a 100-foot complex of buildings, principally a barn and cow house in the grounds of Stokesay farm, then occupied by Herbert Groom. The fire narrowly avoided the castle buildings. Interestingly, the *Illustrated London News* of 1892 still described the castle as partially in ruins and its hall used as farm offices, perhaps confusing the events of 1855 with those of 1890.

Living at 108 Lancaster Gate, London, Allcroft was an absentee owner, leaving the building empty but open to the public. For many years his friend, the Revd John G.D. Le Touché, vicar of Stokesay in 1878, frequently gave guided tours of the castle, which explains this photograph. La Touché is the tall person wearing the frock coat, standing in the centre of the group. When John Allcroft died in July 1893, he left nearly £500,000 in his will, with large bequests to his family and several other people. His eldest son, Herbert John Allcroft, inherited the Stokesay Castle estate.

Fig 116

Figs 117 & 118 Stokesay Castle interiors
Hand-developed gelatin postcard, W.A. Call, c.1910

Two photographic postcards, the top one showing the relative comfort afforded by the solar's seventeenth-century interior, and the bottom one the not-so-cosy, draughty medieval great hall. The lofty timbers of the great hall are contemporaneous with the manor's building date, although there is a suspicion that, after a period of neglect, some may be exacting Victorian replacements.

These suspected replacement timbers may date from 1830 when William, 2nd Lord Craven, made the building watertight by re-roofing or replacing extensive fire-damaged roof sections. The work was later studiously and non-intrusively continued, and further renovations carried out, by its new owner John Derby Allcroft. Today, this wonderful building still has the potential to confound and surprise.

Fig 119 Stokesay Castle gatehouse *Carte de Visite*, Thomas Jones c.1875

The gatehouse to Stokesay Castle was built in around 1640 by William, 1st Earl of Craven. Having lain empty for many years, it was updated in the 1870s to a modern standard for caretaker accommodation.

Fig 120

OPPOSITE: **Fig 120 The Craven Arms Flying Machine**
Hand-developed gelatin postcard, unattributed, c.1906/7

An exciting and rare photograph dating from the beginning of the twentieth century. The riders of the two-person pedal-operated 'aeroplane' with bicycle-parts undercarriage are Samuel Ernest Maund (known as Ernest), bicycle maker/ agent and auto dealer, along with his brother Percy. Samuel operated from premises in Market Street and Station Road, Craven Arms. The improbable flying machine may have been a promotional aid for the business.

Samuel is recorded in 1906 as being in debt to creditors. He was allowed to continue trading, contingent on regular debt repayments being made. He sold the Craven Arms business in 1907, paying off a large portion of the money, moving to a shop in Wem, and later selling this in order to open a business in Shifnal. He went before a registrar for a public examination of his affairs in January 1908, appearing before the Shropshire Quarter Sessions the following April. Accused and found guilty of concealing property while a bankrupt, he was duly sentenced to six months in prison. He later emerged as the proprietor of E. Maund and Sons Ltd, a successful motor engineering business at Day Street Garage, Walsall.

Against this background, an improbable story swirling in myth emerged. Samuel is credited as the first British aviator to achieve flight in a British-built aeroplane in 1907, beating Sir Edwin Roe's and Samuel Cody's flights by 12 months. He is believed by his family to have built a powered aeroplane, not without reason, as they possess various artefacts that support the claim.

A field near Stokesay was used for what was termed an aero club meeting, with tickets sold at 1/- each for people to enter the ground, and a further payment of 3d for children or 6d for adults to view the hidden aeroplane. An aeroplane in flight would have attracted large crowds and been a newsworthy event, but a newspaper record is yet to emerge. The 'flying' exhibition was probably the ground-based pedal-powered 'Craven Arms Flying Machine' being put through its paces as part of a money-making venture by Samuel.

The aero club meeting story is perpetuated in America where, in 2012, Samuel was contentiously lauded in some aviation circles as the first British pioneer aviator. This is supported by a family photograph of an early date (marked 1907) of Samuel and others posing with an aeroplane: 'Britain No 1.'

Malcolm Campbell – father of Donald Campbell of British speed record fame – owned a two-cylinder aeroplane called 'Britain', which proved to be underpowered, and an eight-cylinder 10HP J.A.P. V-Twin engine was retrofitted. In 1910, he could only produce limited hops using the new engine and rid himself of the plane at auction for £22 10s.

Notwithstanding the retrofitting by Campbell, comparison photographs of 'Britain' and 'Britain No1' suggest it to be the same machine. So it appears that Samuel may have purchased the aircraft at auction, perhaps flat-packed for transport and needing reassembling. Although Samuel could build planes of a type, it seems on this occasion that he was the proud owner of a machine built to order for someone else.

Fig 121 Bromfield Priory gatehouse Albumen print, gelatin dry plate, Frith & Co. (image ref. 30844), 1892

From 1836 until 1895 the gatehouse was home to a village school catering for 100 pupils, a large number for a village. The upper-storey school room was also used for entertaining on special occasions when feasts were held for the 90 or so permanent Oakly Park estate workers. The school was rehoused in a new purpose-built school building in 1895, and part of the gatehouse became an estate cottage, while the remainder became the parish reading and recreation room.

Fig 122 Bromfield Sawmill
Albumen stereoview print, collodion wet plate, Thomas Jones, c.1870

A small, water-powered sawmill (note the sawn timber stacked behind the trees on the left and the wall to the right of the mill building). The timber passed through the mill from left to right. The water wheel on the outside powered the blade inside the building. This was driven by water running through the mill race, with the amount allowed through controlled by the sluice gate at the side.

Fig 123 Bromfield Mill
Gelatin postcard, unattributed, c.1915

The second mill at Bromfield, a combined mill house, corn mill and bakery, seen here towards the end of its useful life. The larger of the two mills at Bromfield (with larger mill race and weir), it probably stands on the site of the earlier Priory mill. In 1861, the mill, then occupied by John Dallaway, boasted a weir height of 1.8 metres, three millstones, a separate cottage, several outbuildings and 20 acres of ground. It was next occupied by John Holmes, followed by Mark Evans by 1891.

Fig 124 Bromfield bridge
Glass lantern slide, unattributed, c.1900

A view across the weirs to the eighteenth-century Bromfield bridge, carrying the Oakly Park entrance road. This divides to pass the Pheasantry Covert together with Brick Kiln Covert, and allows a way along the medieval Halton Lane, which eventually joins onto Lower Wood Road/ Dinham Road at Whitcliffe, Ludlow.

The bridge forms a delightful visual complement to the mill and weir complex (the sawmill roof is visible on the right). Otter-hunting and fishing were once part of life on the river here. The *Shrewsbury Chronicle* of September 1901, reported that the Hawkstone Otter Hounds (a local pack) met on Friday at Bromfield bridge to finish the season: 'The weather was fine, and there was a large company present. The hounds were taken down to a point below the Oakly Park Gardens and drew up past the mill and bridge, although no quarry was found'. The *Chronicle* then related how they then went onto the nearby River Onney to continue the day's sport. Fishing was also a regular occurrence on this stretch, with good catches of Grayling often reported.

Figs 125 & 126 Druid Oaks *Carte de visite* photographs, Francis Bedford, 1863–65, (J.P. Getty Museum Collection, courtesy of the Getty open content programme)

In the Middle Ages, Oakly Park was attached to Ludlow Castle as part of its chase, and was probably imparked in the 1500s. By the 1800s the park's many ancient oaks were being called the 'Druid Oaks', probably giving rise to the park's name. Under the title 'The garden party at Oakly Park', the *Shrewsbury Chronicle* of June 1879 described the grounds: 'Through a rock garden, with its cool grotto, aloe trees, abundant ferns, and over an ivy-covered rustic bridge where a group of seven ancient oaks reasoned to have been mentioned in the Domesday book. Highly prized and taken care of by the Clive family, they measure 30 to 40 feet in diameter and were estimated to be 2,000 years old'.

Figs 127 & 128 Downton Castle
Albumen print, collodion dry plate,
Thomas Jones, c.1865

Two fine views of Downton Castle, around ten miles to the west of Ludlow. The parterre seen here was designed by W.A. Nesfield, and adds an air of formality to the scene. Recorded as extant as early as 1862, the garden as laid out here no longer exists. Large terraces are a feature complimenting other views of the house.

The house was built to a design by its owner, Richard Payne Knight in the Gothic revival style between 1773 and 1778. A keen proponent of the picturesque style, he was to bring his love of the 'style of the painter' to the acres of grounds surrounding the house, and commissioned the artist Thomas Hearne to produce a series of drawings of the grounds.

The Second World War saw pupils from Lancing College evacuated to Downton Castle, as Lancing had been appropriated as a naval training facility known as HMS King Alfred (Shore Establishment). Today, Downton Castle is a private home, and not open to the public.

Fig 129 Castle bridge, Downton Castle Albumen print, gelatin dry plate, unattributed, c.1880

The bridge spanning the River Teme is on the southern approach below Downton Castle. One of several carriage drives to the picturesque castle, most became farm tracks. This seems to have been the fate of Castle bridge, as here it can be seen to have fallen into disuse, and is fenced and gated with a rough track beyond. Built of stone in c.1780, it was probably designed by Richard Payne Knight.

Fig 130 Bow bridge Glass lantern slide, unattributed, c.1890

The eighteenth-century packhorse Bow bridge over the River Teme between Burrington and Downton. It was part of the Leintwardine to Ludlow turnpike road in 1780, later becoming a bridleway. The bridge was largely restored in 1980. The River Teme flows through Downton Gorge in a northward direction, but a school of thought now believes that the geology indicates the glacial waters once flowed in the opposite direction, towards the south, perhaps draining through the Aymestry Limestone ridge.

Fig 131 Seven Gables, Orleton Albumen print, gelatin dry plate, unattributed, 1880

The early seventeenth-century timber-framed House of Seven Gables, Orleton, near Ludlow. The photograph shows the rear of the property, its slightly dishevelled yard full of chickens. Called Lower House in 1959, the house is now somewhat altered, and is known as Orleton House.

Fig 132

Fig 132 Bill Poster
Hand-developed gelatin postcard, unattributed, c.1910

Located at least 30 miles from Ludlow is Stourport, where professional bill poster E. Smith's horse and cart, with ladder, was photographed in front of an advertising hoarding in around 1910, by someone unknown. It was subsequently made into a postcard for sale locally – or perhaps for Mr Smith to hand out to customers. As a Ludlow-based tradesman making the long journey to Stourport, Smith was competing with the local bill poster Frederick Landon of Lion Hill. Perhaps for the benefit of prospective customers, the postcard would seem to illustrate that distance was no object when it came to finding customers and space or placing advertising posters. Although in an unknown location within the town, the large hoarding, perhaps temporarily surrounding a building site, would have been a prominent and lucrative space to advertise local and national businesses.

Visible on the hoarding are advertisements for local businesses such as H. Beach, a bicycle manufacturer and agent for the long-established company Rudge Whitworth Bicycles, whose father had run a successful ironmongery business in the town. Pleysey Ltd, another old family ironmongery business, was also advertising Rudge Whitworth bicycles, and there is a Raleigh bicycle advertisement between them, showing the popularity of two-wheeled transport at the time, and the competition between rival manufacturers and sellers. Hedge and Co, a local boot and shoe seller, who by 1912 had ceased trading, is also prominent on the hoarding. The address of an unnamed local auctioneer of 7 Lion Hill can also be seen in the top right of the photograph.

As well as Raleigh, other national companies also feature prominently. Red Bell tobacco was sold by Edward Ringer and Co., a Bristol tobacco manufacturer formed in 1893 by Edward Ringer, who established a business in 1813. Franklyn, Davey and Co. are also prominent. Also visible is an advertisement for Scotland's Dewar's White Label whiskey, created in 1899 for Dewar's by master blender A.J. Cameron at Dewar's new Aberfeldy distillery. John Dewar started trading when he opened a wine shop in 1846, but it was not until 1860 that John began to blend his whiskey at the Tullymet distillery leased by the family business. Now owned by Bacardi, White Label whiskey is still sold today.

∼

References & further information

BOOKS

Beardmore, R., *Ludford House, Ludlow*, Logaston Press, 2020

Gaydon, A.T. et al (eds), *A History of Shropshire* (Victoria County History series), OUP, 1973

Hasluck, P.N. (ed.), *The Book of Photography, Practical, Theoretical and Applied*, Cassell, 1905

Housman, A.E., *A Shropshire Lad*, The Richards Press, 1938

Johnson, A. & K., *Walking the Old Ways of South Shropshire*, Logaston Press, 2019

Leyland J. (1503–52), various antiquarian writings, including about St Laurence's Church, Ludlow

Lloyd, D., *A story of Ludlow Grammer School*, privately printed, Studio Press Birmingham, 1979

Lloyd, D., Clark, M. & Potter, C., *St Laurence's Church, Ludlow*, Logaston Press, 2010

Shepherd, F.G., *The Parish Church of Ludlow*, Jakemans Ltd, 1944

Shoesmith, R. & Johnson, A., *Ludlow Castle. Its History & Buildings*, Logaston Press, 2018

The parish church of St Laurence Ludlow. A monograph of the restoration, 1889–91, George Woolley, Ludlow, 1892

NEWSPAPERS AND MAGAZINES

Birmingham Daily Post 1956
Birmingham Post 1877
Chelmsford Chronicle 1906
Eddowes's Journal, and General Advertiser for Shropshire, and the Principality of Wales 1859, 1860, 1863, 1867, 1875
Globe 1866
Gloucester Echo 1942
Hereford Journal 1860, 1889
Hereford Times 1811, 1843
Illustrated Sporting and Dramatic News 1896
Kington Times 1930, 1956, 1959
Leominster News and North West Herefordshire & Radnorshire Advertiser 1901, 1904, 1906,

London Illustrated News 1886, 1893
Ludlow Advertiser 1838, 1879, 1885, 1890, 1892, 1899, 1900, 1909
Man of Ross and General Advertiser 1879
Motorcycling 1909
Sheffield Evening Telegraph 1912
Shrewsbury Chronicle 1860, 1863, 1901, 1904
Shropshire Star 2010, 2018
Wellington Journal 1895

INTERNET (as at August 2023)
www.abergelepost.com/the-little-flower-of-jesus *A history of Giuseppe Rinvolucri by his son Mario Rinvolucri*
www.britishnewspaperarchive.co.uk *Archive of British newspapers*
www.caynham.eclipse.co.uk/history4.html *Caynham Village History and the Curtis family*
www.francisfrith.com *Francis Frith Collection*
www.getty.edu/art/ *Getty Museum Collection*
www.gracesguide.co.uk/Castle_Foundry,_Ludlow *Grace's Guide To British Industrial Heritage: Castle Foundry, Ludlow*
www.heritagegateway.org.uk/Gateway/ *Listed Building and heritage searches, including Admiral Woodward and Hopton Court*
www.nationalarchives.gov.uk/ *National Archives, including summary of Records of the Botfield Family, 1758–1873, held by the University Manchester Library*
www.oldclassiccar.co.uk/registrations/reg-letters.html *Pre-1973 vehicle registration numbers*
www.shropshirearchives.org.uk *Shropshire Archives*
www.shropshiregeology.org.uk/sgspublications/ *Shropshire Geological Society, including new thoughts on the Origins of Downton Gorge by Kathryn Francis*
www.vam.ac.uk/ *V&A Collections*